Success in Writing

Writing to Persuade

GLOBE FEARON
EDUCATIONAL PUBLISHER
A Division of Simon & Schuster
Upper Saddle River, New Jersey

Executive Editor: Barbara Levadi
Senior Editor: Francie Holder
Project Editors: Karen Bernhaut, Douglas Falk, Amy Jolin
Editorial Assistant: Kris Shepos-Salvatore
Editorial Development: Kraft & Kraft
Production Director: Penny Gibson
Production Editor: Alan Dalgleish
Interior Design and Electronic Page Production: Blue Inc.
Marketing Manager: Nancy Surridge
Cover Design: Leslie Baker, Pat Smythe

Printed in the United States of America
  3 4 5 6 7 8 9 10   99 98 97

ISBN 0-835-91893-9

GLOBE FEARON EDUCATIONAL PUBLISHER
A Division of Simon & Schuster
Upper Saddle River, New Jersey

CONTENTS

UNIT 1 Understanding Persuasion

Writing to persuade is your chance to express your opinions and get others to agree with you! When you talk, you often try to get people to agree with you. For example, you might try to persuade your parents to extend your curfew. To be effective, you would use facts and reasons. You might say, "I'm thirteen now. I think I'm old enough to stay out after ten o'clock." Writing to persuade is just like speaking to persuade. You try to make your readers agree with you.

What to Do

Make persuasion work for you. The purpose of persuasion is to change someone's mind. That purpose is accomplished through a good argument. A good argument shows why opinions, beliefs, or ideas are reasonable.

Use persuasive writing to get things accomplished. Here are two examples.

- You want your school to change the dress code. So you write a letter to the editor of the school newspaper. You persuade the school officials, and other students, that the rules should be changed.

- You think that your friend Miguel should be elected class president. So you write and give a speech. In it, you tell your classmates why Miguel is the best candidate. Then you urge them to do something about it—vote for him!

How to Do It

Follow these guidelines:

State a clear opinion on an issue.
Use facts, examples, and reasons to support the opinion.
Present your argument logically.
Urge readers to think differently or take action.
End on a positive note.

Apply It

▶ Think of uses for persuasion. Make a list of things you would like to accomplish through persuasion. Save your list in your notebook.

CHAPTER 1 Building an Argument

If you were building a house, you would make it strong. First, you would put down a concrete slab or basement. This strong foundation would support your house. Then you might build the body of your house with wood or bricks. Finally, you would finish, or conclude, with the roof.

What to Do

When you write to persuade, you must build an argument. Your argument might take different forms. It might, for example, be an essay, a letter, a speech, or a poster. Whatever its form, give it a solid three-part structure. Give it an introduction, body, and conclusion.

How to Do It

Keep this chart in mind. Here is what you want to do in each of the three parts of a persuasive piece of writing:

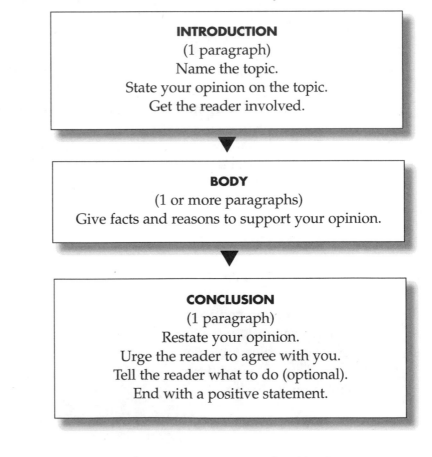

INTRODUCTION
(1 paragraph)
Name the topic.
State your opinion on the topic.
Get the reader involved.

▼

BODY
(1 or more paragraphs)
Give facts and reasons to support your opinion.

▼

CONCLUSION
(1 paragraph)
Restate your opinion.
Urge the reader to agree with you.
Tell the reader what to do (optional).
End with a positive statement.

Review It

▶ What are the three parts of a persuasive piece of writing?

_____

_____

_____

Lesson 1 Beginning with the Introduction

The introduction is the first thing your reader sees. It prepares your reader for the rest of what you have to say. To keep your readers reading, get them involved right away.

What to Do

If your introduction does three jobs, it will be a strong foundation for the rest of your writing. This chart lists the jobs an introduction should do:

> **INTRODUCTION**
> (1 paragraph)
> Name the topic.
> State your opinion on the topic.
> Get the reader involved.

How to Do It

Look at this example. It comes from a letter that a student named Katya wrote to the editor of her school newspaper. Here is the introduction to her letter, as it appeared when it was printed in the paper. It is brief and to the point.

She named her topic. — Take a close look at the school baseball team's uniforms.

She stated her opinion. — The team plays well, but their old uniforms look shabby.

Because we are proud of the team, we should make sure that they look their best!

She got her readers involved.

Review It

▶ Find the sentences that do the three key jobs. Read this introduction to a letter to the editor. On the lines below it, tell which sentences do the three main jobs of the introduction.

> The school library does not have any news magazines. The library should subscribe to some, so that we know what is going on in the world. Today's students need more information than television gives them!

1. Which sentence names the topic?

_____

2. Which sentence states the writer's opinion?

_____

3. Which sentence gets the readers involved?

_____

Lesson 2   Giving Support in the Body

When you have introduced your opinion, support it with facts and examples in the body of your persuasive writing.

What to Do   In the body, write paragraphs that support your opinion. State the reasons for your opinion, and give facts and examples to support it.

> **BODY**
> (1 or more paragraphs)
> Give facts and reasons to support your opinion.

How to Do It   Look at this example. Abdul wrote an essay to support his opinion that *Treasure Island* is a great book. Here is the body of his essay.

There are many reasons why <u>Treasure Island</u> is a great book. First, it is filled with adventure. Jim Hawkins is away from home, sailing on the high seas. He is looking for a treasure that was buried many years ago.

Second, it is filled with danger and suspense. During the voyage, Jim learns that there are rough pirates on his ship. Reading about how Jim outsmarts the pirates and helps his captain find the treasure is exciting.

Finally, <u>Treasure Island</u> makes readers feel that they are part of the story. Jim is about thirteen or fourteen years old. His feelings of fear are so realistic that I could picture every scene in my head, and I could feel exactly the same feelings as Jim.

Abdul gave his opinions. Then he backed them up with facts and examples.

OPINIONS	FACTS AND EXAMPLES
The book is filled with adventure.	Jim Hawkins is sailing on the high seas in search of a treasure.
The book is filled with danger and suspense.	Jim learns that there are dangerous pirates aboard. He must outsmart them.
The book makes readers involved in the story.	Jim's feelings of fear are so realistic that the reader can feel them, too.

Review It

▶ Find the supporting facts in another student's persuasive writing. This student wrote an essay to support the opinion that *Raiders of the Lost Ark* was an exciting movie. Here is the first paragraph of the body of her essay, in which she gives two reasons for her opinion.

There isn't a dull moment in <u>Raiders of the Lost Ark</u>. All by itself, the first scene is filled with thrills and suspense. In that one scene, Indiana Jones finds a golden statue, outsmarts a traitor, and escapes from a collapsing cave. Once outside, he meets a villain who steals the golden statue. Then Jones outruns a band of men who are shooting at him with bows and arrows. He jumps onto a seaplane to get away. That scene is just the opener! The rest of the film is packed with one thrilling conflict after another. For example, Jones must get out of an ancient tomb, filled with dangerous snakes. He must trick a large group of terrible villains. He must even outwit a sneaky monkey!

On the lines below, list the facts and examples that support her opinions.

OPINIONS

FACTS AND EXAMPLES

1. All by itself, the first scene is filled with thrills and suspense.

_____

_____

_____

_____

_____

_____

2. The rest of the film is packed with one thrilling conflict after another.

_____

_____

_____

_____

Lesson 3 Ending with a Strong Conclusion

The conclusion can have different jobs, depending on your purpose for writing.

What to Do

Match your conclusion to your purpose. Sometimes, you just want to make people agree with you on a certain issue. At other times, you want them to take a step further and take an action that shows their support of your opinion. Remember to end your conclusion with a positive statement. It is the last idea that the audience reads. It leaves them with a positive feeling about your views.

> **CONCLUSION**
>
> (1 paragraph)
> Restate your opinion.
> Urge the reader to agree with you.
> Tell the reader what to do (optional).
> End with a positive statement.

How to Do It

Wrap up your argument in three or four sentences. Look at this example. Carl wrote a letter to the editor of a magazine. He wanted to disagree with what he had read in an article. This was his conclusion:

> Therefore, I feel that the article on bike paths was unfair. Bike paths cost money, but I'm sure you and your readers will agree that people in cities need safe places to ride. We can all help by supporting laws to build safe paths. As bike riders, you and I need bike paths—and we all benefit from them!

Carl's conclusion was a strong wrap-up to his argument. Look at what he did:

KEY ELEMENT	CARL'S VERSION
Restate your opinion.	The article was unfair.
Urge the reader to agree with you.	I'm sure you and your readers will agree that people in cities need safe places to ride.
Tell the reader what to do (optional).	You can help by supporting laws to build safe paths.
End with a positive statement.	As bike riders, you and I need bike paths—and we all benefit from them!

Review It

► Find the key elements in two conclusions written by two other students.

Hal wrote a speech. His purpose was to urge other students to wear bicycle helmets. In the body of his speech, he supported his argument with statistics about bicycle accidents and other strong facts. Then, to wrap up, he urged the readers to take an action. Read Hal's conclusion and then answer the questions below it.

> These facts speak for themselves. Bike helmets can save lives. Therefore, wear a helmet! Your life is too important to risk serious injury.

1. Which sentence restates the opinion?

_____

2. Which sentence urges the reader to agree or act?

_____

3. Which sentence ends the speech with a positive statement?

_____

Another student, Raphael, was worried about fund shortages in his school. Foreign language classes were threatened. He decided to speak to a parents' group. He wrote a short speech. Read Raphael's conclusion and then answer the questions below it.

> These examples prove that learning a foreign language is important. Support the teaching of languages in school, and take a foreign language class yourself. You will become a good citizen—not only of your own country, but of the world.

4. Which sentence restates the opinion?

_____

5. Which sentence urges the reader to agree or act?

_____

6. Which sentence ends the speech with a positive statement?

_____

CHAPTER 2 Persuading with Style

When you write to persuade, you want your readers to agree with you. This chapter will show you how the style of your writing can help.

What to Do

Create a persuasive style. In this chapter, you will learn four ways to create a persuasive style:

- Learning How to Sell
- Separating Facts and Opinions
- Showing Respect for the Audience
- Thinking About Opposing Views

How to Do It

To win your readers to your side, appeal to their interests and feelings.

> You will have an unforgettable experience if you join us on the annual class trip.

Use facts when you want to persuade someone to share your views. Your readers may disagree with your opinions, but they cannot disagree with your facts.

> We'll be going to Washington, D. C., which has more public buildings than any other city in the U. S.

Show respect for your readers and their views. If the readers feel that you respect them, they will be more willing to agree with you.

> In the survey, students suggested many other cities, and we'll try to visit those in the future.

Think about the views that you and your readers do not agree on. Find a way to answer their objections before they make them.

> Some people think that the annual class trip is too expensive. This year, we have cut the cost by more than ten percent.

Apply It

▶ Look for examples of persuasive writing in the everyday world. Good places to look include magazines, newspapers, and advertising handouts. Tape or paste them into your notebook. Notice the way each writer has created a persuasive style. If you can, discuss the examples with a partner or group.

Lesson 1 Learning How to Sell

When you write to persuade, you are selling your opinion. Make your readers willing to listen by appealing to their interests and feelings.

What to Do

Ask what the audience wants and needs. Think about your topic from your audience's point of view. Try to put yourself in their position. What do they want? (Remember that it may not be what *you* want.) What do they need? (Remember that it may not be what *you* need.)

How to Do It

Ask yourself key questions about your audience. José Luis, who sells cars for a living, uses this method. He has to persuade each customer to buy a car. He thinks about each customer's feelings.

He asks himself, "What does this person *want* from a car?" If he answers, "performance," he tells the customer about the car's engine.

He asks himself, "What does this person *need* from a car?" If he answers, "good repair service," he mentions that mechanics are on duty twenty-four hours a day.

Review It

▶ Leo wrote a speech urging students to help at a class car wash. Here is part of it. Find the sentences that appeal to the audience's interests and feelings.

> Our class can raise a lot of money for the annual trip at Saturday's car wash. Why sit around with nothing to do next Saturday? Join your friends at the car wash and have fun! The weather will be hot, but the water will be cool, so you can cool off while you work!

1. Which sentence appeals to the need for money for the class trip?

_____

_____

2. Which sentence appeals to the fact that students don't want to be bored?

_____

_____

3. Which sentence appeals to the need to stay cool in hot weather?

_____

_____

Lesson 2   Separating Facts and Opinions

Support your opinions with facts, not with more opinions. Your readers may disagree with your opinions, but they cannot disagree with your facts.

What to Do

Recognize which of your statements are facts and which are opinions. A fact is a statement that can be proved. An opinion is a statement that cannot be proved. It describes a person's feelings. When you write to persuade, you are asking someone to share your opinions on an issue. Show that your opinions are reasonable. Support them with strong facts.

How to Do It

To separate facts from opinions, ask whether a statement can be proved. Think about the "facts" that you plan to use and make sure that they are not just opinions disguised as facts. Look at these facts and opinions to see the differences between them:

Many plants and animals live in rain forests.
Fact: We can check science reports to find out whether it is true.

Everyone should work to save the rain forests.
Opinion: There is no way to prove that everyone should work to save the rain forests. People have other jobs to do.

Rain forests affect the world's weather patterns.
Fact: Science reports will tell us whether it is true.

The rain forests are our most important resource.
Opinion: Some people think that the oceans are more important.

Review It

▶ Find the opinions in a student's writing. Pilar wrote an essay to persuade the school officials to change the dress code. However, she supported her opinion with more opinions. Here is part of the body of her essay.

> The dress code states that students may not wear baseball caps to class. That's really dumb. Many students are sports fans. They should be allowed to wear caps that support their favorite teams. People wear baseball caps outside of school. They should be able to wear them in school, too.

▶ Find and underline each sentence that states an opinion. Then work with a partner or a group to think of facts that Pilar could have used to support her opinion. Write these facts on a separate piece of paper.

Lesson 3 Showing Respect for the Audience

It is important that you show respect for your readers and their views. If the readers feel that you respect them, they will be more willing to agree with you.

What to Do

Find "common ground" between yourself and your readers. The things that you and your readers agree about are called common ground. When you try to find common ground, you search for those views that you and your readers share. Readers will be more willing to agree with your main point if they see that they share other views with you.

How to Do It

Make a Venn diagram. Juan planned to write a letter to the editor of his local newspaper. He hoped to persuade store owners to use paper bags instead of plastic bags. He used this Venn diagram to find common ground with his readers.

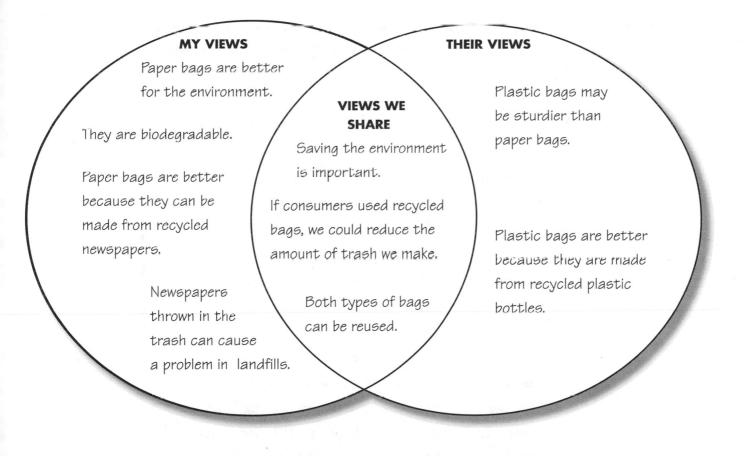

MY VIEWS

Paper bags are better for the environment.

They are biodegradable.

Paper bags are better because they can be made from recycled newspapers.

Newspapers thrown in the trash can cause a problem in landfills.

VIEWS WE SHARE

Saving the environment is important.

If consumers used recycled bags, we could reduce the amount of trash we make.

Both types of bags can be reused.

THEIR VIEWS

Plastic bags may be sturdier than paper bags.

Plastic bags are better because they are made from recycled plastic bottles.

Apply It

▶ Create your own Venn diagram. Suppose that you are planning a letter to the editor of your school newspaper. Your readers are students your age. You want to persuade them to do something. It might be to start a club, or support a school team, or any issue you choose. On a separate sheet of paper, draw a diagram like the one above. Use it to find common ground with your readers. When you are finished, save your diagram for Lesson 4.

Lesson 4 Thinking About Opposing Views

In Lesson 3, you learned how to strengthen your argument by finding common ground with your readers. You also need to think about the views that you and your readers do not agree on.

What to Do

Think about the opposition. When planning to write, ask yourself these questions:

- What might readers say to disagree with me?
- How might they build a good argument against me?

Remember that a strong argument is like a strong building. However, even the strongest building can develop a leak. Look at your argument carefully. Where might the leaks develop? Where might your readers find a strong argument against you?

How to Do It

Think about your readers' objections and answer them before they can object. Juan looked at his Venn diagram that you saw on page 15. He noticed that his readers might have arguments in favor of their views. He decided to show that they were wrong. Here is a paragraph from Juan's letter to the editor. Notice that he provided an argument against opposing views.

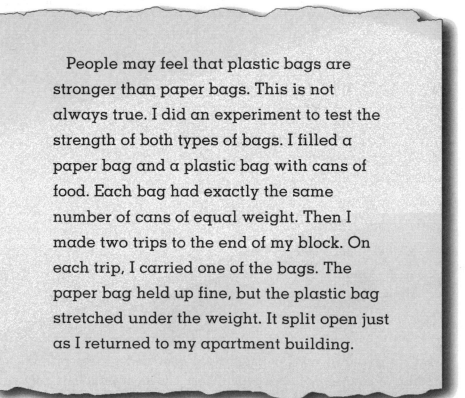

> People may feel that plastic bags are stronger than paper bags. This is not always true. I did an experiment to test the strength of both types of bags. I filled a paper bag and a plastic bag with cans of food. Each bag had exactly the same number of cans of equal weight. Then I made two trips to the end of my block. On each trip, I carried one of the bags. The paper bag held up fine, but the plastic bag stretched under the weight. It split open just as I returned to my apartment building.

Apply It

▶ Use your Venn diagram to find opposing views. Look back at the diagram you made in Lesson 3. Look over the "Readers' Views" section of your diagram. Choose one of the views you listed. On a separate sheet of paper, write a short paragraph. Use facts and reasons to argue against this opposing view.

What Have You Learned in Unit 1?

Use these questions to gather and review your thoughts about the importance of each of the key points in Unit 1. Don't worry about writing complete sentences. Just put some thoughts, ideas, and reactions down for each question.

1. What is writing to persuade?

_____

2. How can you build an argument?

_____

3. What belongs in the introduction to a persuasive essay?

_____

4. What belongs in the body of a persuasive essay?

_____

5. What belongs in the conclusion to a persuasive essay?

_____

6. How can you use style to persuade readers?

_____

7. How can you "sell" your ideas?

_____

8. Why is it important to separate facts from opinions?

_____

9. Why is it important to show respect for your audience?

_____

10. Why is it important to think about opposing views?

_____

▶ If you can, share your answers with a partner or group. Work together to make a list of "Five Great Ways to Persuade a Reader."

UNIT 2 Writing to Persuade

Writing is like walking. You take one step at a time. Writing a persuasive essay may seem like more than you can handle when you first think about doing it. If you break it into steps, each step will seem easier.

What to Do

Follow three basic steps as you write to persuade. In this chapter, you will learn the three basic steps.

- Planning Your Writing
- Developing Your Writing
- Completing Your Writing

How to Do It

Keep this outline in mind. It shows the smaller steps within the three large ones.

Plan your writing.
    Choose a topic.
    Narrow the topic.
    Identify the audience.
    Identify the purpose.
    Gather the facts you need.
    Organize your argument.

Develop your writing.
    Draft the introduction.
    Draft the body.
    Draft the conclusion.

Complete your writing.
    Revise your essay.
    Proofread your essay.
    Publish your essay.

Apply It

▶ Imagine yourself writing to persuade. Begin by looking for examples of persuasive writing in the everyday world. You may already have examples in your notebook from your work on page 12. If not, look in magazines, newspapers, and advertising handouts. Choose one, and imagine that you were writing it. Visualize yourself going through each step. If you can, discuss the steps with a partner or group.

CHAPTER 1 Planning Your Writing

Plan what you want to say. Plan how to say it. You will have a much better chance of persuading your readers if you do.

What to Do

Get your writing off to a good start. When does writing begin? Is it when you start a draft? No, it is earlier than that. Is it when you first make some notes? No, it is even earlier than that. Writing begins as soon as you begin thinking about your topic.

Many of your first ideas will appear in the final draft of your writing. Taking the time to think and plan at the start will make that final draft as good as it can be.

How to Do It

Follow this checklist. In this chapter, you will work through all the steps that are needed to plan a persuasive essay. They are listed in this checklist.

☐ Start by choosing a topic that is important to you. Your essay will be strongest if you collect a few ideas for topics, and then choose the best of them. List topics in your notebook.

☐ Once you have chosen your topic, narrow it until it fits your assignment and the space and time available to you. Use a topic web.

☐ Think about the people who will read your finished essay. To persuade them to agree with you, you must make sure that they understand what you are saying. Complete audience profile forms.

☐ Decide what your purpose for writing is. The basic purpose of a persuasive essay is to get your audience to agree with you. You might also ask them to do something once they agree with you.

☐ Gather the facts you need to back up your opinions. Arguments based only on feelings or opinions are weak. To strengthen your argument, you must back up opinions with facts. Use a sources chart.

☐ Organize your argument so that your reader will understand it and find it convincing. Use a planning chart.

Apply It

▶ As you complete the lessons in this chapter, return to this page to check off each step above. You will be able to see the progress you are making.

Lesson 1   Choosing a Topic

The best persuasive essays are about issues the writers really care about. So, start by choosing a topic that is important to you. Your essay will be strongest if you collect a few ideas for topics and then choose the best of them.

What to Do

To find topics for a persuasive essay, ask yourself these questions:

1. What issues in the news or in my community do I have very strong feelings about? (Examples might be new laws, concerns about the environment, concerns about civil rights.)

2. What issues at school do I have very strong feelings about? (Examples might be rules about being on a team, dress codes, or the types of after-school programs that are offered.)

To choose your best idea for a topic, ask these questions about your list:

Which issue do you care about most?
Which idea could you best support with strong facts and reasons?

How to Do It

Look at this example. A student named Nadia chose to explore Question 2. She jotted down these ideas for changes she would like to see at school. She decided that she felt most strongly about the "every practice" rule for school athletes. She checked that one.

Student athletes should be tested for drug use.

✔ Players should not have to come to every practice in order to play on teams.

In-line skating should be allowed on the track at lunch time.

Students should be able to leave school at lunch time.

Kids should be allowed to wear baseball caps to class·

Apply It

▶ In your notebook, or on a separate sheet of paper, jot down some ideas about issues that you have strong feelings about. Place a check mark next to the best idea.

Lesson 2 Narrowing a Topic

Once you have chosen your topic, narrow it until it fits your assignment and the space and time available to you.

What to Do
Focus on one important idea. Narrowing a topic means focusing on one part of it. Suppose you have been assigned to write an essay of three paragraphs. The topic "Why Math Is Important," is too large, or broad. You wouldn't be able to cover it in just three paragraphs. You might narrow it down to "Math Skills Can Lead to Great Careers." That topic could be handled well in three paragraphs.

How to Do It
Use a topic web. Nadia used a topic web to explore her topic. First, she wrote her topic in the central block. Then, in the circles, she jotted down her ideas about her topic.

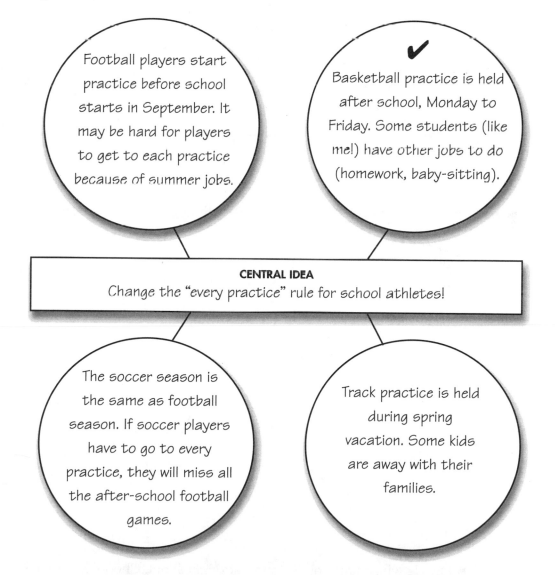

Football players start practice before school starts in September. It may be hard for players to get to each practice because of summer jobs.

✔
Basketball practice is held after school, Monday to Friday. Some students (like me!) have other jobs to do (homework, baby-sitting).

CENTRAL IDEA
Change the "every practice" rule for school athletes!

The soccer season is the same as football season. If soccer players have to go to every practice, they will miss all the after-school football games.

Track practice is held during spring vacation. Some kids are away with their families.

Nadia saw that four ideas would not fit in her essay. She focused on just one of them. She chose to write about basketball because it meant most to her. She narrowed her topic to "Change the every-practice rule for basketball players."

Apply It   ▶ Use this web to narrow your topic. Write your topic in the central block. Write your ideas in the circles. Add as many circles as you need to write all your ideas.

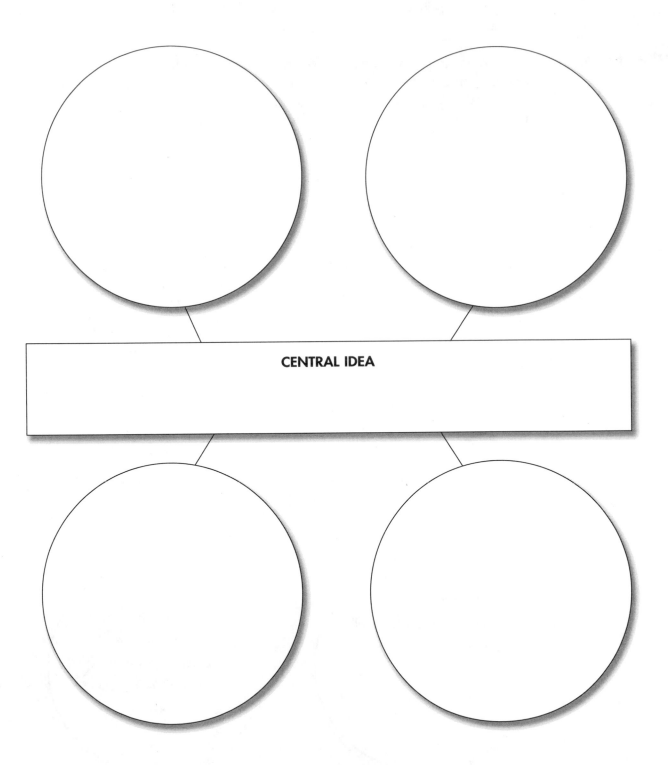

CENTRAL IDEA

▶ Decide which idea you feel most strongly about. Choose one to develop. Rephrase your topic to match the choice you have made. Save the other ideas for other essays.

Lesson 3 Identifying the Audience

The readers of your finished essay are called your audience. To persuade your audience to agree with you, you must make sure that they understand what you are saying.

What to Do

Before you write, think about who your readers are. Decide the following things about them:

- their ages and positions
  (Are they classmates or are they younger students? Are they adults, such as the school principal or a teacher?)
- what they already know about your topic
- what they might need to know to understand your topic fully
  (What facts should you provide?)
- what special interests they have regarding your topic
  (How can they benefit from agreeing with you?)

How to Do It

Make an audience profile. Before Nadia began to write her essay, she took some time to think about her audience. She had two different audiences in mind. She thought of writing to other members of the basketball team. She also thought about writing to the school principal, Dr. Brock.

Nadia made a profile for each audience. She compared them. Then she made her choice. She decided that she would choose Dr. Brock as her target audience. This is the profile she made for Dr. Brock:

NARROWED TOPIC: Change the every-practice rule for basketball players.

AUDIENCE: Dr. Brock

AGE RANGE/POSITION: adult; principal of school

KNOWLEDGE REGARDING TOPIC: knows we have a basketball team; knows that there is an every-practice rule

---

OTHER FACTS THEY MAY NEED TO KNOW: may not know that we have practice every day after school; does not know why I have to miss practice on Tuesdays (Mom's new job, my need to baby-sit my brother Claude); does not know how much basketball means to me

---

INTERESTS REGARDING TOPIC: may be concerned about changing a rule; may not want to make suggestions to the coaches

---

Apply It

▶ Think of possible audiences for your persuasive essay and choose one as your target audience.

▶ First, think of two possible audiences. Use the following forms to make a profile for each one.

NARROWED TOPIC:
AUDIENCE:
AGE RANGE/POSITION:
KNOWLEDGE REGARDING TOPIC:
OTHER FACTS THEY MAY NEED TO KNOW:
INTERESTS REGARDING TOPIC:

NARROWED TOPIC:
AUDIENCE:
AGE RANGE/POSITION:
KNOWLEDGE REGARDING TOPIC:
OTHER FACTS THEY MAY NEED TO KNOW:
INTERESTS REGARDING TOPIC:

▶ When you have finished your profiles, work with a partner if you can. Talk about the audiences you have profiled. Decide which one you would most like to reach. Choose that one audience for your persuasive essay.

Lesson 4 Identifying the Purpose

Your purpose for writing is your goal. It is what you want your writing to accomplish. The basic purpose of a persuasive essay is to get your audience to agree with you. You might also ask your audience to do something once they agree with you.

What to Do

To identify your purpose, answer these questions:

1. What opinion do you want to state? Identify your topic and your point of view.

2. Why do you feel strongly about your topic? Answer with strong facts and reasons that will convince the audience to agree with you.

3. What do you want the audience to do? Urge them to agree and, perhaps, to take some action to show that they agree.

How to Do It

Look at the way Nadia answered the three questions. She jotted answers to the questions in her notebook. The answers helped her focus on her purpose for writing.

> Narrowed topic: Change the every-practice rule for basketball players.
>
> Audience: Dr. Brock
>
> 1. My opinion is that the every-practice rule is sometimes unfair or hard to follow.
> 2. I feel strongly about this because I'm a good player, and I work hard, but I can't come to practice every day. Practice is held every day, and I have to baby-sit on Tuesdays.
> 3. I want Dr. Brock to agree with me and talk to the coaches about changing the rule.

Apply It

▶ Answer the three questions above about your purpose for writing. Write your answers in your notebook.

▶ If you can, discuss your purpose with a partner or group. Help one another think of ideas for accomplishing the purpose each of you has identified.

Lesson 5 Gathering Information

Arguments based only on feelings or opinions are weak. To strengthen your argument, you must back up opinions with facts.

What to Do   Find facts to support your opinions. You want to tell your readers what you think, of course. Do not stop there, though. Tell them why you think as you do. Give them reasons for your opinions. Find the facts you need to show that your opinions make sense.

How to Do It   Use this chart. It will help you decide where to look for the facts you need.

TO FIND FACTS ABOUT . . .	TRY THESE SOURCES . . .
SCHOOL ISSUES	school newspaper interviews with students, teachers, and staff members research about other schools your own experiences

NEIGHBORHOOD AND COMMUNITY ISSUES	local newspapers
	local libraries
	interviews with neighbors, friends,
	    and community leaders
	your own observations
	    and experiences

NATIONAL OR WORLD ISSUES	newspapers and news magazines encyclopedias and almanacs television and radio reports data from computer on-line services

Nadia used the chart to think of sources for her facts about a school issue. She decided to use her own experience, interviews with other students, the school newspaper, and interviews with students and coaches at other schools.

Apply It   ▶ Get the facts you need. Look back at the chart of sources. On a separate sheet of paper, jot down specific sources for the facts you need to support your argument. Use these sources to gather your facts. Make sure that you take careful notes as you use each of your sources.

Lesson 6 Organizing Information

You have found the information you need to support your argument. Now it is time to organize that information.

What to Do Follow these hints:

- Your introduction can be as short as three sentences. First, identify the topic. Then, state your opinion. Finally, give the major reason for your opinion.

- To plan the body of your essay, list all the facts you will use to support your opinion. Build your argument carefully, saving your strongest fact for last.

- Plan to keep your conclusion to two or three sentences. Make your point. Then ask your audience to agree with you. If you want to urge them to act, tell them what you would like them to do. End with a positive statement.

How to Do It Use a planning chart. Here is the one that Nadia used to get her ideas organized.

She identified the topic. —— Members of the basketball team are required to attend every practice.

She stated her opinion. —— That rule should be changed.

She gave her major reason. —— The rule is hard to follow for players with after-school commitments.

Next, Nadia listed all the facts she would use to support her opinion. Then she numbered the facts in the order in which she would present them in her essay.

Notice that she saved the strongest and most important fact for last.

> **2** I have to baby-sit Tuesday afternoons.
> **1** Players have basketball practice every day.
> **4** The Kane School has no every-practice rule. They won the state championship.
> **5** Players might get more practice time if we split into groups and practiced on different days of the week.
> **3** My friend Kim had to stop taking trumpet lessons on Monday afternoons. She had to choose between her trumpet lessons and the basketball team.

Here are the notes Nadia made to help her plan the conclusion to her essay. First, she planned how to urge Dr. Brock to agree with her. Then she planned what action she would suggest to Dr. Brock.

> I urge you to think about changing the every-practice rule.
> I suggest that you talk about the problem with Coach DiNardo and perhaps hold a meeting with the coach and players.

Apply It

▶ Complete this planning chart. Use the chart to organize your thoughts on your topic. Jot some notes in the boxes. Make changes until you are satisfied with your plan.

INTRODUCTION

Make your argument clear.

State your topic.

State your opinion.

BODY

Make your argument strong.

List the facts and reasons you will use for support.

Number the facts to show the order in which you will use them.

Save your strongest fact for last!

CONCLUSION

Get your readers to do something to show their support.

Urge them to agree with you.

Suggest an action they should take.

CHAPTER 2 Developing Your Writing

As you write your drafts, work from your plan. Keep your audience and purpose in mind. Make your writing do its job.

What to Do

Get your ideas on paper.

Each version of your writing is called a draft. To get the first draft on paper, start writing wherever it is easiest for you to begin. Maybe you will want to copy a sentence from your notes.

Do not worry about spelling or grammar right now. Just get your ideas down on paper.

How to Do It

Follow this checklist. In this chapter, you will work through all the steps that are needed to develop a persuasive essay. They are listed in this checklist.

☐ Draft the introduction. To start your essay with strength, open with a hook. A hook is a strong statement or question that grabs the reader's interest right away. Be sure to mention your topic. State your opinion. Give your most important reason for holding that opinion.

☐ Draft the body. You identified your topic and gave your opinion in the introduction. Now support that opinion in the body of your essay. Use facts, reasons and examples. Show that your opinion makes sense.

☐ Draft the conclusion. Like your introduction, your conclusion should be brief and to the point. You have already stated your opinion and supported it with strong facts and reasons. Now it is time to bring your argument to a strong close. Tell your readers what you want them to do.

Apply It

▶ As you complete the lessons in this chapter, return to this page to check off each step. You will be able to see the progress you are making.

Lesson 1 Drafting the Introduction

To get your essay off to a strong start, begin with a hook. A hook is a strong statement or question that grabs the reader's interest right away.

What to Do   Follow these hints:

- Use your notes as a guide as you write.
- Start with a hook to grab the reader's interest. Turn your topic statement into a question or make it surprising.
- Following the hook, identify your topic and state your opinion. Be brief and to the point.
- If you are not sure how to express your opinion strongly and clearly, just do the best you can. Later, after you have written the body, you can go back and make some changes.
- Do not worry about spelling and grammar right now. You will have time to proofread your work later.
- If you get stuck, save the introduction for later. Go on to the next lesson, and begin to draft the body of your essay. Once the body is finished, the introduction may be easier to write.

How to Do It   Look at this example. You saw Nadia's notes in her planning chart on page 27. She used the topic statement from those notes to write a hook.

First, she started with her topic statement.
— Members of the basketball team are required to attend every practice.

Then she turned it into a question.
— Why should members of the basketball team be required to attend every practice?

Finally, she made the question more surprising.
— What makes a great basketball player—perfect shots or perfect attendance?

Then she went on to finish her introduction. She used the notes from her chart.

What makes a great basketball player—perfect shots or perfect attendance at practice? The basketball team's every-practice rule should be changed. The rule is hard to follow for many players.

Apply It   ▶ On a separate sheet of paper, draft the introduction to your essay. Look at the notes that you took in the introduction part of the planning chart on page 28. In those notes, you identified your topic. Now turn your topic statement into a hook. Then state your opinion. Finally, give your most important reason for holding that opinion.

Lesson 2 Drafting the Body

In your introduction, you identified your topic and gave your opinion. Now support that opinion in the body of your essay.

What to Do

Follow these hints:
- Use your notes as a guide as you write.
- Present your facts and reasons in the order that you decided upon on page 28. Save your strongest fact or reason for last.
- If you are not sure that the order you chose is really the strongest order, follow your plan for now. Later, you can revise the body of your essay and move sentences around if you want.
- As you write, keep your audience and purpose firmly in mind. Think about your readers' special interests and concerns.
- Do not worry about spelling and grammar right now. Just get your facts down on paper! You will have time to proofread later.

How to Do It

Study this example. This is the draft of the body of Nadia's essay.

She appealed to the interests of her audience, Dr. Brock. She thought that Dr. Brock might be concerned that without the rule, players might skip practices for no important reason.

> The players on our team have practice every day of the week. New rules should be made. The rules should say that players with important after-school commitments could miss a few practices and still be on the team.
>
> Many players have other commitments. My mother needs me to baby-sit on Tuesday afternoons, so I have to miss practice. My friend Kim used to take trumpet lessons on Monday afternoons. She had to choose between her trumpet lessons and the basketball team. She chose basketball. I think that she should be allowed to do both.

She saved her most important point for last.

> The Kane School basketball team has no every-practice rule. Maybe how <u>hard</u> a player practices is more important than how <u>often</u>. Players could focus better and practice harder if they knew they didn't have to give up other commitments to be on the team.

Apply It

▶ On a separate sheet of paper, write a first draft of the body of your essay. Use the notes that you took in the body part of the planning chart on page 28.

Lesson 3 Drafting the Conclusion

Like your introduction, your conclusion should be brief and to the point. You have already stated your opinion and supported it with strong facts and reasons. Now it is time to bring your argument to a strong close.

What to Do

Follow these hints:

- Use your notes as a guide as you write.
- Restate your opinion.
- Urge the audience to agree with you or suggest an action they might take.
- End with a strong, positive statement.
- Do not worry about spelling and grammar right now. Focus on writing a strong ending to your essay. You will have time to correct any errors later.
- If you have trouble writing the conclusion, go back and work on the introduction some more. The introduction and the conclusion work together. The introduction gets your argument started. The conclusion finishes it. Go back and forth between them. You will find that one gives you ideas for the other.

How to Do It

Look at this example. It is Nadia's conclusion. Notice that it is brief and to the point. She used only four sentences.

First, she restated her opinion. Then she urged Dr. Brock to agree with her. She suggested an action for Dr. Brock to take. Finally, she ended with a strong, positive statement. The positive statement is very important. It is the last idea that the audience reads, and it ends the essay with a pleasant mood and feeling.

> For these reasons, I think that the every practice rule should be changed. I hope you will agree. I urge you to talk with Coach DiNardo about the problem and then plan a meeting with the coach and the players. Together, we can improve the rule and have a great basketball team!

Apply It

▶ On a separate sheet of paper, write a draft of the conclusion to your essay. Use the notes that you took in the conclusion part of the planning chart on page 28.

CHAPTER 3 Completing Your Writing

When the first draft is written, return to it to make it better. Revise it to make it stronger. Proofread it to make it correct. Then publish it to bring it to your audience.

What to Do

Make your writing better with every draft.

Revise the first draft to make a second draft that is better.

Keep working at your drafts until your writing says just what you want to say as well as you can say it. Draft, revise, and revise again until you are pleased with your work.

How to Do It

Follow this checklist. In this chapter, you will work through all the steps that are needed to complete a persuasive essay. They are listed in this checklist.

☐ Revise your essay. Now that you have your ideas down on paper, it is time to go back and revise. When you revise, you make changes to make sure that you have expressed your ideas clearly. Read your draft carefully. Use the revision checklist on page 35 to correct and strengthen your writing.

☐ Proofread your essay. Fix any mistakes in spelling, grammar, and punctuation. Read your revised draft sentence by sentence and word by word, looking for the little mistakes that you might have missed or ignored earlier. Use the proofreading checklist on page 36 to find and correct any mistakes.

☐ Publish your essay to bring it to your audience. Choose a way of publishing that will bring your ideas to your audience's attention. Follow the requirements of the method you choose.

Apply It

▶ As you complete the lessons in this chapter, return to this page to check off each step. You will be able to see the progress you are making.

Lesson 1 Revising Your Essay

Now that you have your ideas down on paper, it is time to go back and revise. When you revise, you make changes to improve what you have written.

What to Do

Make improvements in your work.

Start by reading what you have written. Don't make changes now. Just read.

Then read it again. This time, begin making changes. Use the revision checklist on the next page to guide your work. Keep making changes until your writing says just what you want to say as well as you can say it. Above all, make sure that you have expressed your ideas clearly.

How to Do It

Look at this example. Nadia used the revision checklist as she revised her draft. Here is a portion of her revised essay, showing some of the changes she made.

She cut words to make the hook shorter and give it more impact.

She rewrote this sentence to stress that the rule is unfair to students with after-school commitments. She also wanted to show that the students and the team suffer.

She rewrote this sentence so that she would sound reasonable, not angry.

She cut words that were not needed.

She made this sentence more active.

What makes a great basketball player—perfect shots or perfect attendance ~~at practice~~?
The basketball team's every-practice rule should be
It keeps students with after-school commitments off the team.
changed. ~~The rule is hard to follow for many players.~~
   The players on our team have practice every day
   I think that the   **changed**
of the week. ~~Now~~ rules should be ~~made~~. The rules
should say that players with important after-school
commitments could miss a few practices
and still be on the team.
   Many players have other commitments.
My mother needs me to baby-sit on Tuesday
afternoons, so I have to miss practice. My friend Kim
~~used to take trumpet lessons on Monday afternoons.~~
~~She~~ had to choose between her trumpet lessons and the
basketball team. She chose basketball. I think
      the rules should allow her
that ~~she should be allowed~~ to choose both.

Apply It

▶ Use this revision checklist to guide you as you revise your work.

Introduction:
- ☐ Open with a hook. If you did not, add a hook now. If you did, make sure that it grabs the reader's attention.
- ☐ State the topic clearly in the introduction. If you have not, add a sentence now. If you have, try to make the statement clearer.
- ☐ State your opinion clearly and strongly. If you have not, add a sentence now. If you have, try to make the statement clearer and stronger.
- ☐ Tell your main reason for your opinion. If you have not done it, do it now. If you have, try to make the reason clearer and stronger.

Body:
- ☐ Use facts and examples to support your opinion. If you have not done it, add facts and examples now. If you have, check them to be sure they are correct.
- ☐ Do not try to support opinions with other opinions. If you did, replace the opinions with facts.
- ☐ The facts must be clear to your audience. If they do not seem clear, explain them.
- ☐ Put related facts and examples in paragraphs of their own. If each group does not have its own paragraph, divide the body into smaller paragraphs.
- ☐ Put the paragraph with the strongest facts and examples in last place. If you did not, move it there now.
- ☐ Show that you respect your audience's opinions. If you did not, add a sentence now to show that you do.
- ☐ Answer objections that your audience may have. If you did not, do that now.

Conclusion:
- ☐ Your conclusion should be brief. If it is not, see what you can cut. If it is brief, make sure that it says everything it should say.
- ☐ Urge your readers to agree with you. If you did not, add a sentence now. If you did, make sure you wrote a sentence that your readers will like.
- ☐ You may have urged your readers to take action. If you did, make sure that they will think the action is reasonable. If you did not, decide whether you would like to urge them to take action now.
- ☐ End the essay with a strong, positive statement. If you did not, add one. If you did, make sure that the words you used will give the audience positive feelings.

General:
- ☐ Do not use bland words, such as *great*, *good*, or *nice*. Replace them with stronger, more specific words.
- ☐ Do not leave grammar errors in your essay. Correct any that you find. You will take a closer look when you proofread.

▶ If you can, work with a partner to revise your work. Read each other's drafts. Use the revision checklist to find places that might be improved. Make helpful suggestions to improve each other's work. Think about your partner's suggestions for your essay. Make the final decisions yourself about what to change.

Lesson 2 Proofreading Your Essay

Now it is time to fix any mistakes in spelling, grammar, and punctuation. Follow these steps for proofreading your essay.

What to Do

When you proofread, look for the little mistakes that you might have missed or ignored earlier.

When you are writing a draft, you should focus on getting your ideas down. When you are revising, you should focus on improving the meaning of your work.

Now it is time to look for mistakes in grammar and spelling. Read your work sentence by sentence and word by word. Use the Proofreading Checklist below to find and correct any mistakes.

How to Do It

Use the following checklist. It lists problems you may find in persuasive writing. You also will find a guide to grammar, mechanics, and usage on pages 76–80.

Grammar:
☐ Subjects and Verbs: Make sure that all subjects agree with their verbs in number. (Singular subjects need singular verbs. Plural subjects need plural verbs.)
☐ Complete Sentences: Make sure that all of your ideas are in complete sentences. Correct any fragments.
☐ Pronouns: Make sure that you have used pronouns correctly. Is it clear what noun each pronoun refers to?
☐ Adjectives and Adverbs: Use adjectives to modify nouns or pronouns. Use adverbs to modify verbs, adjectives, and other adverbs.

Punctuation:
☐ To end sentences: Make sure each sentence ends with a period, question mark, or exclamation point.
☐ In contractions: Make sure that you have placed apostrophes correctly in all contractions to show where letters have been taken out.
☐ To separate items in a series: Use commas to separate three or more items in a series (*apples, oranges, and pears*).

Spelling:
☐ Check the essay for spelling errors. If you are unsure about the spellings of certain words, use a dictionary. Be especially careful about the spellings of people's names.

Apply It

▶ Use the proofreading checklist to find errors in your work. Correct them. If you can, work with a partner. A fresh eye may see errors that you overlooked.

Lesson 3 Publishing Your Essay

You have worked hard to prepare and polish your essay. Now take it to your audience!

What to Do   Find the best way to reach your audience.

How will you publish your essay? How can you be sure that your audience will see it or hear it? If you can, discuss ideas with a group of students. Consider everyone's suggestions, and then choose the plan that you feel is right.

How to Do It   Choose a way of publishing that suits your audience. Here are some suggestions.

Audience	Ways to Publish
students or adults at school	an article, editorial, or letter in the school newspaper a poster in the library or cafeteria a flyer sent to classrooms a speech on the school intercom a letter to the one person you want to reach
people in your neighborhood or city	an article or letter to the editor of a local newspaper a poster in a community center a flyer delivered to homes a speech at a neighborhood center a spot on a local radio station or cable television station

Nadia chose to publish her essay as a letter that she delivered to Dr. Brock's office.

Apply It   ▶ Publish your essay in the way you choose. Find out what rules you must follow. For a newspaper, for example, find out the editor's name. Find out how to get your essay into the editor's hands. Find out whether there are guidelines for length. Remember, too, that most papers have deadlines you must meet.

What Have You Learned in Unit 2?

Use these questions to gather and review your thoughts about the importance of each of the key points in Unit 2. Don't worry about writing complete sentences. Just put some thoughts, ideas, and reactions down for each question.

1. Why is it important to choose a topic that you feel strongly about?

_____

2. Why is it important to narrow your topic?

_____

3. Why is it important to identify the audience you are going to try to persuade?

_____

4. Why is it important to describe your specific purpose?

_____

5. Why is it important to gather facts to support your opinion?

_____

6. What should you put in the introduction of a persuasive essay?

_____

7. What should you put in the body of a persuasive essay?

_____

8. What should you put in the conclusion of a persuasive essay?

_____

9. What do you do when you revise?

_____

10. What do you do when you proofread?

_____

▶ If you can, share your answers with a partner or group. Share the ideas and experiences you had. Since writing is always filled with unexpected twists and turns, talk about what was funny or strange about the experience, too. Come up with a group list called "Tips for Writing Persuasive Essays."

UNIT 3 Writing on Your Own

There are many types of persuasive writing. You may be familiar with some, such as advertisements and speeches. They have different forms, but their goals are similar. They are written to get readers to agree with the writer's opinion or to take action.

What to Do

Become familiar with the three different kinds of persuasion that you will write in this unit:

A Letter to the Editor
A Speech Urging Action
A Letter of Complaint

How to Do It

Learn the key elements of each kind that you will write.

A letter to the editor is written to be published in a magazine or newspaper. Most often, it is a response to an article. The writer has read an article that made him or her react strongly. The writer uses persuasive skills to "talk back" to the article writer.

A speech is meant to be spoken or read aloud. The writer wants to capture an audience and hold their attention. Most often, the speech is a response to an issue or situation that made the writer want to act. The writer uses persuasive skills to urge people to do something about the issue.

A letter that states a consumer complaint is written by a customer to complain about a poor product. It might be written to the company that made the product. It might be written to a store where the product was bought. The writer has a definite goal. He or she wants a refund or a new product. The writer uses persuasive skills to get satisfaction.

Apply It

▶ Find examples of each of the types of persuasion you will write in this unit. Look for letters to the editor in the letters columns of magazines and newspapers. Look for speeches in newspapers and on television. You can also find books of speeches at a library. Look for letters of complaint in consumer magazines. You can also find them in magazines about particular interests. For example, a magazine about music may have letters of complaint about stereo equipment. Save the examples in your notebook.

CHAPTER 1 Writing a Letter to the Editor

Have you ever read an article in a magazine or newspaper that made you laugh or made you really angry? You do not have to keep your feelings to yourself. Use your skills as a persuasive writer. Write a letter to the editor!

What to Do
Notice what is unique about a letter to the editor. For one thing, a letter to the editor is indeed a letter. It is written to be published in a magazine or newspaper. Most often, it is a response to an article.

How to Do It
Look at this example. It is a letter that a student named Angela wrote to *Outdoor Sports* magazine. The parts of her letter are labeled.

SALUTATION

INTRODUCTION
Tell what article you are responding to. State your position.

BODY
Back up your position with reasons and facts.

CONCLUSION
Tell the readers what you think. Tell them what they should do. End with a positive statement.

CLOSING

Dear Editor:

As a mountain bike rider, I enjoyed "Will Mountain Bikes Kill the Mountains?" by Ted Stone. However, I disagree with Stone. He stated that all bike riders harm the mountains. The members of the Mud Riders Club do not harm the mountains!

All Mud Riders members must uphold the club's "rules of the trail." We do not use trails where biking is not allowed. Never do we leave trash in the woods. We always ride in a way that will not endanger others. We work hard to protect the mountains we love.

I urge all mountain bike riders to join or form a club like ours. You can help save the mountains, and you can have fun doing it.

Sincerely,
Angela Mendez

Review It

1. In the introduction, what opinion does Angela state?

_____

2. In the body, what is one fact that she uses to support her opinion?

_____

3. In the conclusion, what does Angela suggest that her readers do?

_____

Lesson 1   Choosing a Topic

Look through some newspapers and magazines. Find articles that excite you, make you angry, or make you laugh. Which article stands out from the others? Respond to that article in your letter to the editor.

What to Do

Focus on one point. If your letter is too long, it probably will not get printed. So plan to keep your letter brief. Decide on one important point that you want to make. If you make that one point clearly and strongly, you will have a good chance of seeing your letter in print.

How to Do It

Use an idea branch to focus your thinking. Here is the one that Angela used.

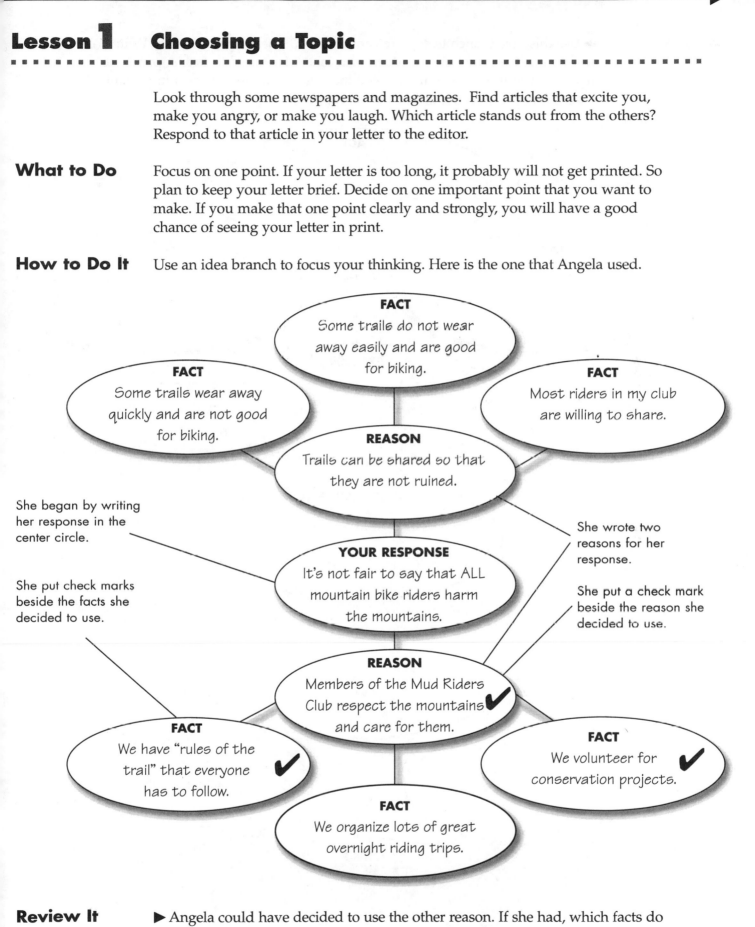

She began by writing her response in the center circle.

She put check marks beside the facts she decided to use.

FACT
Some trails do not wear away easily and are good for biking.

FACT
Some trails wear away quickly and are not good for biking.

FACT
Most riders in my club are willing to share.

REASON
Trails can be shared so that they are not ruined.

YOUR RESPONSE
It's not fair to say that ALL mountain bike riders harm the mountains.

She wrote two reasons for her response.

She put a check mark beside the reason she decided to use.

REASON
Members of the Mud Riders Club respect the mountains and care for them. ✔

FACT
We have "rules of the trail" that everyone has to follow. ✔

FACT
We volunteer for conservation projects. ✔

FACT
We organize lots of great overnight riding trips.

Review It

▶ Angela could have decided to use the other reason. If she had, which facts do you think she could have used? Put check marks beside them.

Apply It

▶ Use this idea branch to explore and focus your ideas for your letter. Write your response in the center circle. Add your reasons. Then add facts to support the reasons. Add more circles if you need them. Then choose the most important reason and the most important facts to support it.

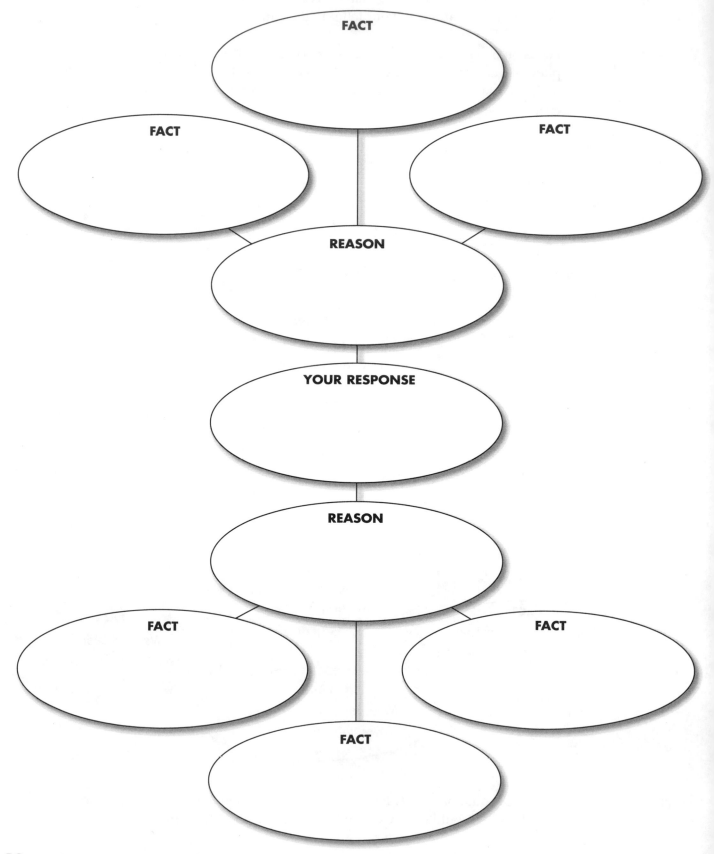

Lesson 2 Organizing Your Ideas

A letter to the editor contains the three main parts of a persuasive essay: the introduction, body, and conclusion. The letter must be short, so each part must be short, too.

What to Do

Follow these hints to organize your letter.

Begin the introduction with the salutation. Plan to keep your introduction to three sentences. First, identify the article. Then sum up the idea you are responding to. Finally, state your position.

Plan to keep the body to one paragraph. Get right to the point. Support your position with the reasons you jotted down in Lesson 1. Back up those reasons with your facts. Build your argument carefully, saving your strongest fact for last.

Plan to keep your conclusion to two or three sentences. Make your point. Then ask your readers to agree with you. If you want to urge them to act, tell them what you would like them to do. End with a positive statement. Add a closing to your letter and sign your name.

How to Do It

Use a letter planning chart . Here is the one that Angela used.

INTRODUCTION

She identified the article.

She summed up the idea she was responding to.

She stated her position.

She cut ideas that she didn't need.

> ~~I've been reading Outdoor Sports for years.~~
> I read "Will Mountain Bikes Kill the Mountains?"
> Ted Stone said mountain bike riders harm the mountains.
> I don't agree.
> ~~I usually like Ted Stone's articles.~~

BODY

She supported her opinion with facts.

She cut a point that would have needed more facts to back it up.

She cut ideas that would make her letter too long.

> I'm a member of Mud Riders.
> We've got important "rules of the trail":
> • Do not use trails where biking is not allowed.
> • Do not leave trash in the woods.
> • Do not ride dangerously.
> ~~We volunteer for conservation projects.~~
> ~~Most members of my club want trails for bikers only.~~
> ~~Some trails wear away quickly. Some don't.~~
> ~~Ones that do wear away: use for hiking only.~~
> ~~Ones that don't wear away: use for biking only.~~

CONCLUSION

She made her point.

She urged her readers to agree.

She urged them to act.

She ended with a positive statement.

She cut an idea because it went with the idea she had cut from the body.

> Every bike rider should join a club like ours.
> Form a club of your own.
> Help save the mountains.
> Have fun doing it.
> ~~There are enough trails for hikers AND bikers.~~
> ~~Start sharing now!~~

Apply It

▶ Use this letter planning chart to organize your thoughts on your topic. Jot some notes in the boxes. Make changes until you are satisfied with your plan.

INTRODUCTION
Because you are writing a letter, start with the salutation. In the introduction, tell what article you are responding to. State your position.

BODY
Back up your position with reasons and facts.

CONCLUSION
Tell the readers what you think. Perhaps urge them to take an action. End with a positive statement. Add the closing and your name.

Lesson 3   Writing Your Letter to the Editor

You are off to a good start! Now you are ready to write your letter to the editor.

What to Do   Use your notes to write the draft of your letter. Use the checklists on the next page to help you revise and proofread it.

How to Do It   Look at this example. It is Angela's draft. Notice how she used the revision and proofreading checklists to make improvements and fix mistakes.

She rephrased a sentence.

She strengthened her main point.

She corrected a spelling mistake.

She cut details that did not really support her main point.

She strengthened her positive statement.

She remembered to follow the closing with a comma.

Dear Editor:

As a mountain bike rider, I enjoyed "Will Mountain

Bikes Kill the Mountains?" by Ted Stone.

disagree with Stone   **stated**
However, I ~~don't agree~~. In the article, he ~~says~~ that all

bike riders harm the mountains. The members of the

do not harm the mountains!
Mud Riders Club ~~don't~~.

All Mud Riders members must uphold the club's

"rules of the trail." We do not use trails where biking is

not allowed. Never do we leave trash in the woods.

others
We always ride in a way that will not endanger. We

protect
work hard to ~~portect~~ the mountains we love. ~~We also have~~

~~lots of fun. Every year we organize overnight trips.~~

I urge all mountain bike riders to join or form a club

You can help save the mountains,
like ours. ~~Save the mountains! Have fun!~~

and you can have fun doing it!
Sincerely ,

Angela Mendez

She added a missing quotation mark.

She chose a stronger and more formal word.

She added a needed apostrophe.

She added a word to make this point clearer.

Apply It

▶ On a separate sheet of paper, write your draft. Use the notes you made on page 44. Do not worry about spelling and grammar right now. Focus on drafting a strong, direct letter.

After you have written the draft, read it. Then revise it. Use the checklist on page 35 and the one below, which focuses on key elements of a letter to the editor.

When you have revised your draft, proofread it to find and fix any mistakes in spelling, capitalization, punctuation, and grammar. Use the checklist on page 36 and the one below, which lists problems to be especially careful about in a letter to the editor.

Revision Checklist
- ☐ Open your letter with a salutation.
- ☐ Name the article you are responding to.
- ☐ State your opinion about the article.
- ☐ Support your opinion with facts.
- ☐ Keep your letter brief. Cut details that do not really support your position.
- ☐ Make your final statement positive.
- ☐ End your letter with a complimentary close.

Proofreading Checklist
- ☐ Check the spellings of people's names.
- ☐ Check the spelling and wording of the title of the article you are responding to.
- ☐ Use capital letters for proper nouns and proper adjectives.
- ☐ Put a colon after the salutation.
- ☐ Put a comma after the complimentary close.
- ☐ Check the guide to grammar, mechanics and usage on pages 76–80.

If you can, revise and proofread with a partner. Use the checklists to think of ways to improve your letters. Listen to your partner's suggestions.

Once you have revised and proofread your own letter, make a clean copy of your letter. Follow the rules for business letters. You will find them on page 57.

Look in the front section of the magazine or newspaper to which you plan to send your letter. Find the address for letters to the editor. Then send your letter in! You could also send it to the editor of your school paper or to a friend or relative who shares your interest in the topic.

CHAPTER 2 Writing a Speech Urging Action

Think of a time when an issue or situation made you want to act. You might have said to yourself, "Something must be done about this!" You can urge people to take action. Write a strong speech that gets results!

What to Do

Notice what is unique about a speech urging action. Remember that most speeches are spoken or read aloud. A speech must be interesting and direct. You want to capture your audience and hold their attention.

How to Do It

Look at the key elements of this speech that a student named Juan wrote. It follows the basic format of a persuasive essay. It has an introduction, a body, and a conclusion.

SALUTATION
Identify and address your audience.

INTRODUCTION
Start with a hook that grabs the interest of your audience. Then identify your topic and state your position.

BODY
Back up your position with reasons and facts.

CONCLUSION
Tell the readers what you think. Tell them what they should do. End with a positive statement.

> Fellow students:
> Once there were so many fish in Napoli Creek that I caught a prize-winning trout. Today there are no more fish in Napoli Creek. Pollution has killed them. We have to fight the pollution and clean up our creek!
> Factories along the creek have dumped chemicals into it. Once the water was clear. Now it is cloudy. Is it any wonder that the fish have disappeared?
> I urge you to join me in cleaning the creek. Work with me to get the city government to make the factories follow clean-water laws. Volunteer to help clean up the litter. Together, we can bring back our creek!

Review It

▶ Identify the key elements in Juan's speech.

1. In the introduction, what position does Juan take?

_____

2. In the body, what is one fact that Juan gives to back up his position?

_____

3. In the conclusion, what does Juan urge his audience to do?

_____

Lesson 1   Gathering Ideas

What issues or situations at school or in your city concern you? It might be an environmental issue. It might be a law or a school rule that you disagree with.

What to Do   Explore your feelings on the issues. Think about issues or situations that you feel strongly about. If you can, meet with a group of students. Talk about issues. Discuss ideas for speeches. Then, on your own, choose one idea for the topic of your speech.

How to Do It   Use an idea web to explore your feelings on your topic. Here is an idea web that Juan created. Juan began by putting his topic in the central box. He used the outer circles to note some reasons why he felt strongly about his topic.

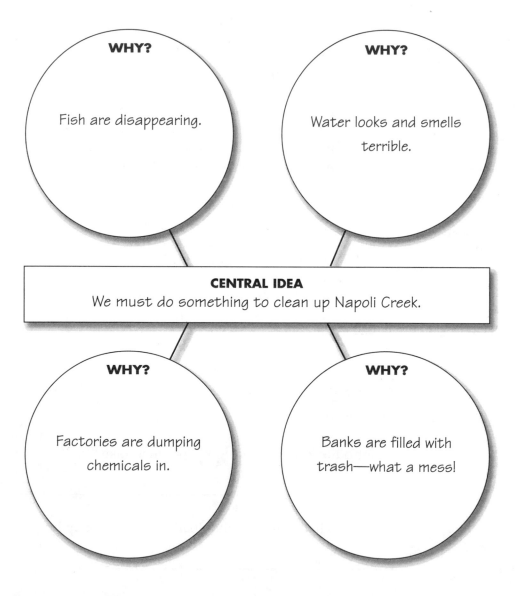

WHY?

Fish are disappearing.

WHY?

Water looks and smells terrible.

CENTRAL IDEA
We must do something to clean up Napoli Creek.

WHY?

Factories are dumping chemicals in.

WHY?

Banks are filled with trash—what a mess!

Apply It   ▶ On a separate sheet of paper, make an idea web like Juan's. Use it to summarize your topic and note some reasons why you feel strongly about your topic. Add more circles if you need them.

Lesson 2 Backing Up Your Position

Facts make the strongest support to an argument because facts can be proved. Your audience cannot disagree with your facts.

What to Do

Use facts to support your opinions. Your idea web from Lesson 1 may contain both facts and opinions. You need facts to support opinions. You can, of course, use opinions as support too. You might get an opinion from an expert, or one from someone who is involved in the issue or situation. Opinions can provide helpful support. Remember, though, that your audience can disagree with them.

How to Do It

Use a fact and opinion chart. Juan used the chart below to add details to support his position. He also used the chart to make sure he understood the difference between what was a fact and what was an opinion.

Juan began by summarizing his position.

He jotted down opinions. He crossed out those that he thought were weak or unrelated to his position.

He listed facts that he would use to support his opinions. Each one could be proved true.

Topic
Clean up Napoli Creek!

Opinions	Facts, Reasons, Examples
Catching fish in the creek used to be great fun.	Fish are disappearing and dying.
The water smells terrible.	Factories have dumped chemicals into the creek.
~~The water looks really gross!~~	The water used to be clear, but now it's cloudy brown.
~~People who throw litter in public places should be fined!~~	The banks are littered with trash.
The banks were much prettier when the grass was there.	The grass along the banks and in shallow water has died.

Apply It

▶ Make a fact and opinion chart to list the facts and opinions that you might use to support your position. When you are finished, look over your work carefully. Can all your facts be proven true? Are any of your opinions weak or unrelated to your main position? Make all the necessary changes until you are satisfied that your facts and opinions create strong support. Then save your chart for use in Lesson 3.

Lesson 3 Planning the Action

A speech urging action ends by—you guessed it—urging the audience to *do* something.

What to Do

Plan what you will ask your audience to do to support your position. Remember to keep the action reasonable. Do not give them an assignment that they cannot do!

How to Do It

You can use an idea web to plan reasonable actions to suggest. Here is one that Juan used. Note that he jotted down all his ideas. Then he crossed out those that seemed unreasonable.

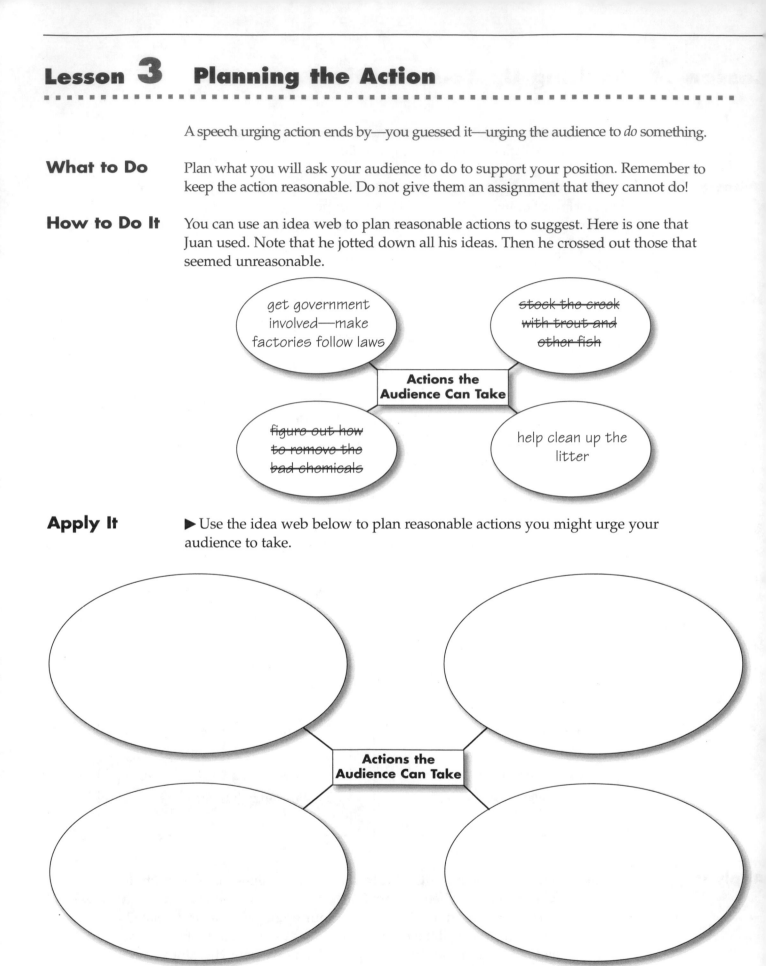

Apply It

▶ Use the idea web below to plan reasonable actions you might urge your audience to take.

Lesson 4 Drafting Your Speech

In the drafting stage, the point is to get your words on paper. Focus on *what* you want to say. You can improve the *way* you say it later.

What to Do   Give your speech an introduction, a body, and a conclusion.

How to Do It   You can begin at the beginning and work right through the draft. This is one way to write a draft. If it doesn't work for you, start somewhere else. Many writers like to start with the body. They write the introduction later.

Draft the Introduction
Begin your speech with a salutation, which identifies the audience.
(For example: "Fellow students . . .")
Follow the salutation with a hook.
> Look back over your fact and opinion chart from Lesson 3.
> Which fact or opinion stands out? Circle it.
> Turn it into a hook.
State your topic.
State your position on your topic.

Draft the Body
Present your opinions, facts, and reasons.
> Look over your fact and opinion chart.
> Number the facts and opinions from weakest to strongest.
> Save your strongest point for last. (That is probably the one you used to create a hook.)
> Be sure that you have support for every opinion.
> If you don't, add a sentence of support now. You can always improve it later.

Draft the Conclusion
Restate your position on the topic.
Ask your audience to agree with you.
Urge your audience to take some reasonable action.
> Use your idea web from page 50.
End with a strong positive statement.
> If you can base it on your hook, it will be even better.

Apply It   ▶ On a separate sheet of paper, draft your speech, using the notes and plans you have made. Do not worry about spelling and grammar right now. Get your ideas down on paper.

Lesson 5 Completing Your Speech

Remember that a speech is meant to be spoken—and *heard*. As you revise, pay close attention to how your speech will sound.

What to Do   After you have written the draft, read it and revise it. Then proofread it to find and fix any mistakes in spelling, capitalization, punctuation, and grammar.

How to Do It   Use the revision checklist on page 35 and the one below, which focuses on key elements of a speech urging action. Use the proofreading checklist on page 36 and the one below, which lists problems to be especially careful about in a speech.

Revision Checklist
- ☐ Open your speech with a salutation.
- ☐ Use a hook to get your audience's attention.
- ☐ Name the issue you are going to discuss.
- ☐ State your opinion about the issue. Be sure that your opinion is clear.
- ☐ Support your opinion with facts. Add facts if you can. Replace weak ones with stronger ones.
- ☐ Be sure that your audience will understand how the facts support your opinion.
- ☐ Keep your speech brief. Cut details that do not really support your position.
- ☐ Urge your audience to take action. Make sure that the action is reasonable.
- ☐ Make your final statement positive.

Proofreading Checklist
- ☐ Check the pronunciation of every name.
- ☐ Check the pronunciation of every word that you are not really sure of.
- ☐ Check the guide to grammar, mechanics, and usage on pages 76–80.

Apply It

▶ If you can, revise and proofread with a partner. Read your speeches aloud. Listen for places that are confusing. Listen for arguments that are not convincing. Suggest ways to improve each other's speeches and correct errors. Finally, when you are satisfied that your speech is the best it can be, make a clean copy.

▶ Hold a "speaking out" session with your classmates. Have students present their speeches. Talk about their issues, their positions, and what they have urged their audience to do.

Have you ever bought a product and been disappointed with it? A piece of clothing may have shrunk, or a game might have had missing pieces. You can use your persuasive writing skills to protect your rights as a consumer!

What to Do You can write a letter stating a consumer complaint. That is a business letter written by a buyer to complain about a poor product. It might be written to the company that made the product. It might be written to a store where the product was bought.

How to Do It A letter of complaint has a definite goal. The writer wants the reader to do something. Often, that is to refund the money paid or send a new product. Here is a letter that a student named Cora wrote. The letter follows the basic format of a persuasive essay. It has an introduction, a body, and a conclusion.

RETURN ADDRESS
This is Cora's address.

DATE

INSIDE ADDRESS
This is the company's address.

SALUTATION
Identify and address your audience.

INTRODUCTION
Identify the product. Give information about your purchase. Identify what you have enclosed as proof of your purchase. State your complaint.

BODY
Back up your complaint with reasons and facts.

CONCLUSION
Ask the audience to agree with you. Urge them to take specific action. End with a positive statement.

COMPLIMENTARY CLOSE
Use a formal closing, such as "Yours truly," followed by a comma. Sign your name on a separate line.

> Cora Washington
> 40 Elm Street
> Dayton, Ohio 15534
> July 1, 1996
>
> Customer Service Department
> Corco Company
> 11 Sam Houston Plaza
> San Antonio, Texas 90876
>
> Dear Customer Service Department:
>   On May 12, I bought a Corco portable stereo at Scott's Store in Dayton, Ohio. It is model #4123. I have enclosed a copy of my sales slip. I am dissatisfied with the stereo because the cassette recorder does not work.
>   I followed the directions in the owner's manual that came with the stereo to record from the FM radio. However, when I rewound the tape and played it, nothing had been recorded on it. I have tried this process many times, always with the same results.
>   I'm sure you will agree that this is a serious problem. Please send me a refund for the full amount I paid for my stereo or tell me how to return it for replacement. My friends have always told me that Corco stereos are the best. I look forward to becoming a satisfied customer.
>   Yours truly,
>   *Cora Washington*
>   Cora Washington

Review It

1. Circle the words that tell what product Cora bought.
2. Circle the words that tell where she bought it.
3. Underline the sentence that tells what proof of purchase she enclosed.
4. Underline the sentence that summarizes her complaint.
5. Underline the sentence that tells what action she urged the company to take.

Lesson 1　Backing Up Your Complaint

It is not enough to complain. You must show that you have a good reason for complaining.

What to Do

Show the company that your complaint is reasonable. To back up your consumer complaint, you must follow two important rules:

1. Prove that you bought the product. Make a photocopy of your sales slip or other proof of purchase. Mention it in your introduction and enclose it with your letter.

2. Back up your complaint with strong facts. You cannot simply say, "I didn't like your product. Send my money back." You must be truthful, polite, and complete. Use facts and reasons to explain why you are unhappy with the product.

How to Do It

Take one step at a time. First, think about the main reason behind your complaint. Here are a few examples of problems you may have with certain products.
- It broke (for example, a toy, tool, or watch).
- Pieces are missing (for example, a puzzle or kit).
- It wore out too quickly (for example, clothing or a tool).
- It doesn't run properly (for example, a stereo or hair dryer).

Then use a fact and opinion chart to jot down notes about the main reason for your complaint. Here is a fact and opinion chart that Cora used.

Complaint
The cassette recorder doesn't work.

Opinions	**Facts, Reasons, Examples**
I should get my money back or a new stereo. The stereo isn't worth what I paid for it. Corco products should run properly!	I followed the directions. Red light came on to show recording was starting. Tape started to turn. Light went off. Tape stopped turning. When tape was rewound, it was blank.

Be careful when you use opinions to back up a consumer complaint. Because you are a dissatisfied customer, your opinions will probably be negative. You do not want to offend the company. Instead, you want to persuade the company to care about your problem and do something to fix it. Keep your letter strong and positive by relying on facts. Notice that Cora decided not to use one of her opinions.

Apply It

▶ Use a fact and opinion chart to plan your letter. When you have finished your chart, save it for use in Lesson 2.

Lesson 2 Organizing Your Ideas

A letter of complaint contains the three main parts of a persuasive essay: an introduction, body, and conclusion. Remember that it must be in business letter form.

What to Do

Begin the letter with the salutation.

In the first sentence of the introduction, name the product. Include a model number or model name if there is one. Then tell where and when you bought the product. Mention the proof of purchase that you are enclosing. End the introduction with a sentence that states your main complaint.

For the body, look at your fact and opinion chart. List the facts and opinions in the order in which you will present them. Save your strongest point for last.

In the conclusion, urge the company to agree with you. Suggest a reasonable action for the company to take. End with a positive statement. Remember that you want to get the company on your side.

How to Do It

Look at this example. It is the letter planning chart that Cora used to organize her ideas.

INTRODUCTION
She found the model number on the back of the stereo.

> I bought a Corco portable stereo.
> May 12, Scott's Store, Dayton, Ohio
> Model #4123
> Copy of sales slip enclosed.
> Cassette recorder does not work.

BODY
She decided that she did not have to give so many details. It would be enough to say that she followed the directions.

> I followed the directions in the owner's manual to record from the FM radio.
> ~~I pushed both the "play" and "record" buttons, as directed.~~
> ~~The red light came on.~~
> ~~The cassette tape was turning as it was supposed to.~~
> ~~After about a minute, the red light flickered off.~~
> ~~Then the cassette tape stopped turning.~~
> Nothing had been recorded.
> I tried this many times, with the same results.

CONCLUSION
She suggested two actions that the company could take.

She ended with a positive statement.

> This is a serious problem.
> Please send me a refund for the full amount.
> Replacing it would be all right, too.
> My friends tell me that Corco stereos are the best.
> Please make me a satisfied customer.

Apply It

▶ Use this letter planning chart to organize your thoughts for your letter of complaint. Jot some notes in the boxes. Make changes until you are satisfied with your plan.

INTRODUCTION
Start with the salutation. Name the product, including a model number if appropriate. Tell where and when you bought it. Mention the proof of purchase that you are enclosing. State your main complaint. (Use your fact and opinion chart.)

BODY
List the facts you will use from your fact and opinion chart. Number the facts in the order in which you will present them. Save your strongest point for last.

CONCLUSION
Urge the company to agree. Suggest a reasonable action for the company to take. End with a positive statement.

Lesson 3 Drafting Your Letter of Complaint

Remember that a letter that states a consumer complaint is a business letter. Therefore, you should use formal, polite language.

What to Do

Use the notes you have made to write the draft of your letter.

How to Do It

This checklist lists all the steps to follow in writing a draft of your letter.

To open the letter in business letter form:
- ☐ Write your return address.
- ☐ Write the date.
- ☐ Write the inside address, naming the person or department you are writing to, the company, and the company's address. The address should be listed on the product or its packaging.
- ☐ Write the salutation, followed by a colon.

To draft the introduction, use your letter planning chart and:
- ☐ Name the product.
- ☐ Include a model number or name if appropriate.
- ☐ Tell where and when you bought it.
- ☐ Mention the proof of purchase that you are enclosing.
- ☐ State your main complaint.

To draft the body, use your letter planning chart and:
- ☐ Write the facts in the order that you numbered them.
- ☐ Save your strongest fact for last.

To draft the conclusion, use your letter planning chart and:
- ☐ Urge the company to agree.
- ☐ Suggest an action for the company to take.
- ☐ End with a positive statement.

To close the letter in business letter form:
- ☐ Write the complimentary close, followed by a comma.
- ☐ Sign your name. (When you make a final, typed copy of your letter, you will type your name and then sign your name above the typed name.)

Apply It

▶ Use the checklist to draft your letter. As you complete each part, place a check mark in the box.

Lesson 4 Completing Your Letter of Complaint

Now for the final step: Complete your letter and send it off. If you have persuaded the company that your complaint is reasonable, you should get satisfaction.

What to Do

After you have written the draft, read it. Then revise it. and proofread it. Finally, when you are satisfied with your letter, type or write it neatly and sign it.

How to Do It

Use the revision checklist on page 35. Use the proofreading checklist on page 36. Also use the checklists below, which focus on key elements and proofreading problems in a letter of complaint.

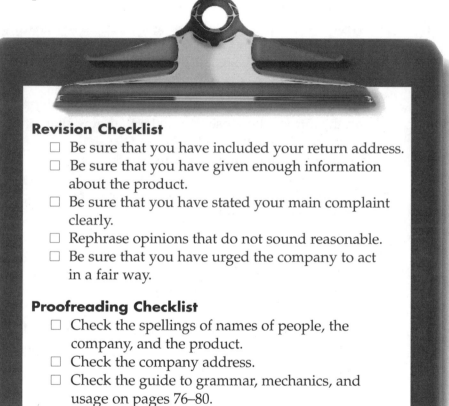

Revision Checklist

☐ Be sure that you have included your return address.
☐ Be sure that you have given enough information about the product.
☐ Be sure that you have stated your main complaint clearly.
☐ Rephrase opinions that do not sound reasonable.
☐ Be sure that you have urged the company to act in a fair way.

Proofreading Checklist

☐ Check the spellings of names of people, the company, and the product.
☐ Check the company address.
☐ Check the guide to grammar, mechanics, and usage on pages 76–80.

Apply It

▶ Go through all the checklists. When your letter is ready, prepare an envelope. Stamp it, mail it, and look forward to a response!

In the upper left corner, print or type your name and return address.

Cora Washington
40 Elm Street
Dayton
Ohio 15534

Copy the inside address onto the center of the envelope.

Customer Service Department
Corco Company
11 Sam Houston Plaza
San Antonio, Texas 90876

What Have You Learned in Unit 3?

Use these questions to gather and review your thoughts about the writing you did in Unit 3. Don't worry about writing complete sentences. Just put some thoughts, ideas, and reactions down for each question.

Letter to the Editor

1. Why does a person write a letter to the editor?

_____

2. What topics are best for a letter to the editor?

_____

3. What should you do in the conclusion of a letter to the editor?

_____

Speech Urging Action

4. What is the purpose of a speech urging action?

_____

5. What should you do in the introduction of a speech urging action?

_____

6. What should you do in the conclusion of a speech urging action?

_____

7. How should you prepare a speech for presentation?

_____

Letter of Complaint

8. What is the purpose of a letter of complaint?

_____

9. What form should you use for a letter of complaint?

_____

10. What facts should you include in a letter of complaint?

_____

▶ If you can, share your answers with a partner or group. Share the ideas and experiences you had. Talk about problems you had while writing. Talk about your successes, too. Develop a group list of tips for each kind of writing you did in this unit.

UNIT 4 Writing on Assignment

Sometimes, you will be told what to write. You will be given an assignment. This is true of adult writers, too. In all types of careers, people have writing to do as part of their jobs. Often, their writing assignments have deadlines. A deadline is the time when a writing project must be completed. To meet a deadline, you may have to shorten some of the writing steps.

What to Do   Become familiar with the two different kinds of persuasion that you will write in this unit:

> A Test Essay
> An Advertisement for a Product

How to Do It   Learn the key elements of each kind that you will write.

A test essay is unique in two important ways.

First, it is written in response to a question or a set of directions. You have to make sure that you answer the question or follow the directions.

Second, a test essay is written under a deadline. You must work as quickly and efficiently as possible. You must organize your thoughts quickly. You must limit your answer to what you can write before the deadline. You will not have much time to revise. You will be able to make only the most important changes.

An advertisement has one main purpose: to persuade the audience to buy the product. For that reason, thinking about the audience is especially important.

Writers in the advertising business know that they must direct their ads to their target audience. They identify the likely buyers. Then they create ads that will appeal directly to the wants, needs, and interests of those people. To persuade that audience to buy, they provide details about the product. They choose words carefully to present those details in the most positive way.

Apply It   ▶ Find examples of each of the types of persuasion you will write in this unit. Look for advertisements in magazines. Look for an essay you have written for a test. If you can, work with a group to discuss how the writers of the examples (including you) have persuaded their audiences. Save the examples in your notebook.

Many tests in English classes include essays. Often, a test will ask you to read a statement and then write a persuasive essay in which you agree or disagree with the statement. Your teacher will expect you to support your opinion with strong facts and reasons.

What to Do

A test essay follows the standard format of all persuasive essays. It has an introduction, a body, and a conclusion. However, a test essay is unique. Most often, it is written in response to a prompt. A prompt is a question or a set of directions. Here is a sample test prompt.

> Read this statement by an English author named Richard Steele. Explain the meaning of the statement. Then tell whether you agree or disagree. Support your opinion with facts and reasons.
>
> "Reading is to the mind what exercise is to the body."

How to Do It

Study this example. It is a test essay that a student named Ralph wrote in response to the prompt above.

Notice that Ralph first explained the meaning of the statement. Then he stated that he agreed with it. Next, he supported his opinion with facts and reasons. In his conclusion, he restated his opinion. Finally, he ended his essay with a summarizing statement of his point of view.

INTRODUCTION
Tell what the statement means. State your opinion.

BODY
Support your opinion with facts and reasons.

CONCLUSION
Restate your opinion. End with a summarizing statement of your point of view.

> Richard Steele's statement means that reading exercises the brain the way that physical activity exercises the body. I agree with this statement.
>
> It is a well-known fact that sports and exercises make the body strong and healthy. In a similar way, reading makes a person's mind stronger and healthier. Through books, we can gain knowledge about the world. We can learn about foreign lands and distant planets. We can also gain new ideas about government and religion. New ideas help people to grow. New ideas make us more intelligent.
>
> For these reasons, I agree with Richard Steele. Reading can be extremely helpful to a person's growth and intelligence.

Review It ▶ Answer the following questions about the essay that Ralph wrote.

1. What other facts and reasons might Ralph have used to support his opinion?

_____

_____

_____

_____

_____

2. What facts and reasons might Ralph have used to disagree with Steele's statement?

_____

_____

_____

_____

_____

Apply It ▶ Practice your persuasive writing skills. Use facts and reasons to tell why you agree or disagree with Ralph's point of view.

_____

_____

_____

_____

_____

_____

_____

_____

Lesson 1   Understanding the Prompt

Most test essays have to be planned and written quickly. You have only a certain amount of time before the test period is over. Therefore, you must organize your thoughts as quickly as possible.

What to Do The first step in writing a great test essay is to focus on the prompt. Decide exactly what it asks you to do or tells you to do. Those are your reasons for writing.

How to Do It Study the prompt from Ralph's essay test as an example. Note the key words that Ralph underlined.

> Read this statement by an English author named Richard Steele. <u>Explain the meaning of the statement.</u> Then <u>tell whether you agree or disagree. Support your opinion with facts and reasons.</u>
>
> "Reading is to the mind what exercise is to the body."

Ralph analyzed the prompt to understand the assignment. He found the key words *explain*, *tell*, and *support*. These words showed him that the prompt was telling him to do three things:

1. Explain the meaning of the statement.
2. Tell whether he agreed or disagreed.
3. Support his opinion with facts and reasons.

Review It 1. Read this prompt. Underline key words and phrases that tell what the purpose for writing is.

> Read this statement by American author Willa Cather. In your own words, summarize what it means. State whether you agree or disagree. Use facts and reasons to support your point of view.
>
> "Most of the basic material a writer works with is acquired before the age of fifteen."

Study the key words that you have underlined in the test prompt. List the three steps in this writing assignment.

2._____

3._____

4._____

Lesson 2 Organizing Your Thoughts Quickly

When you answer a test prompt, you must limit your answer to what you can cover in a few paragraphs. You do not have much time, so you have to get organized quickly.

What to Do

Use the prompt as the outline for your answer. Your list of the key steps in answering the prompt is your outline. If a section of the outline needs support, make a cluster diagram. A cluster diagram can help you focus and limit your ideas.

How to Do It

Study this example. These are the notes that Ralph made.

First, Ralph jotted some notes to sum up Steele's meaning (step 1 of his purpose).

Next, he stated his opinion (step 2 of his purpose).

Then, he made a quick cluster diagram to gather notes for facts and reasons to support his opinion (step 3 of his purpose).

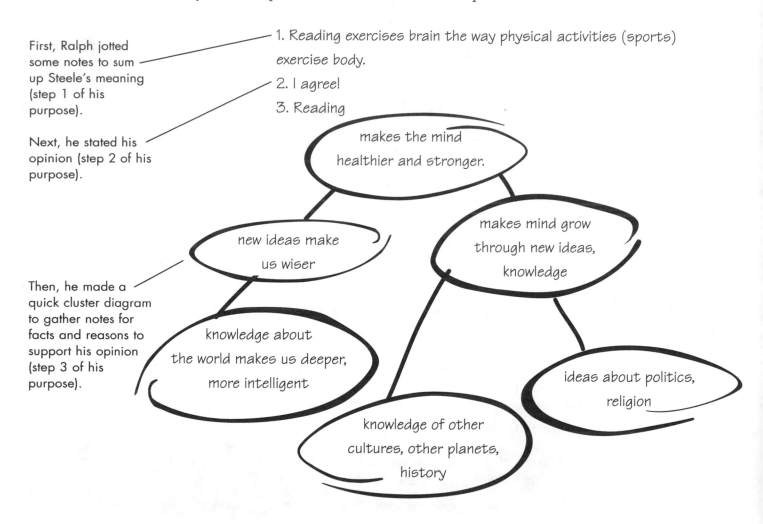

1. Reading exercises brain the way physical activities (sports) exercise body.

2. I agree!

3. Reading

makes the mind healthier and stronger.

new ideas make us wiser

makes mind grow through new ideas, knowledge

knowledge about the world makes us deeper, more intelligent

knowledge of other cultures, other planets, history

ideas about politics, religion

Review It

▶ Look back at the test prompt that you analyzed on page 63. On a separate sheet sheet of paper, quickly make an outline and a cluster diagram to focus and organize your ideas. Give yourself a time limit of 5 to 10 minutes.

Lesson 3   Drafting Under a Deadline

A deadline is a writer's term for the date or time when a writing project must be completed. To meet a deadline, you may have to shorten some of the writing steps.

What to Do
Adapt to the deadline. When you are writing a test essay, you are writing under a deadline. You may have only thirty minutes to an hour to complete your essay. Therefore, you must work as quickly and efficiently as possible.

How to Do It
These tips will help you to get organized and draft your test essay.

Organizing

- Quickly make a cluster diagram, as you did in Lesson 2. Look it over. Make sure that it is clear and complete.

- Number the facts and reasons in the order in which you will present them. NOTE: Recall that in persuasive writing, you often save your strongest fact or reason for the end. However, for this type of essay, you might want to *begin* with your strongest fact or reason. If time runs out, you will have completed the strongest part of your argument.

Drafting

- Do not let the time pressure get to you. Relax. You have analyzed the prompt and made complete notes. The most difficult part of the writing assignment is actually over.

- Write or print as neatly as possible. Because this is a test, you probably will not be able to make a fresh, final copy of your essay.

- Skip a line between each line of writing. This will leave you space to make revisions and proofreading once your draft is complete.

- Follow these steps to complete your draft as quickly as possible. Refer to the items on your cluster diagram as you write.

  - Introduction
    Sum up the statement's meaning.
    State your opinion.

  - Body
    Use facts and reasons to support your opinion. Present them in the order in which you numbered them on your cluster diagram.

  - Conclusion
    Restate your opinion. (For these reasons, I agree, disagree . . .)
    If you wish, end with a statement that summarizes your point of view.

Apply It   ▶ Use this test prompt to practice planning and drafting your persuasive test essay. If you wish, set a time limit for yourself so that you can practice writing under a deadline. Allow yourself 30 minutes in total to answer the question. Spend 5 to 10 minutes planning and organizing. Spend about 15 minutes writing the draft. That should leave you 5 to 10 minutes to revise and proofread in Lesson 4.

First, read the prompt. Then read the beginning of one student's response to it. You can use it as the beginning of your response.

Read this statement by American author Willa Cather. In your own words, summarize what it means. State whether you agree or disagree. Use facts and reasons to support your point of view.

"Most of the basic material a writer works with is acquired before the age of fifteen."

Willa Cather's statement means that writers use more childhood experiences than adult experiences in their writing.

▶ On a separate sheet of paper, jot notes and organize them. Finally, write a draft of your answer below.

_____

_____

_____

_____

_____

_____

_____

_____

_____

Lesson 4 Completing a Test Essay

When you are working under a deadline, you will not have time to make all the changes you would like to make. Make the most important ones first. Those are the ones that affect the *meaning* of your work.

What to Do Finish the draft of your essay before your time is up. You want to have enough time left in the test period to go over it quickly.

How to Do It Because you are taking a test, you will not be able to revise and proofread with a partner. Make any changes that you feel will improve your test essay. Write or print as neatly as possible, making it clear where words and phrases should be inserted. Rely on your own good judgment, and use these checklists for help.

Revision Checklist
- ☐ Check your explanation of the statement. If it is not clear, use simpler words. If it is not complete, add to it.
- ☐ State your opinion clearly. One sentence should be enough.
- ☐ Use strong facts and reasons. If they seem weak, look for stronger ones in your notes.
- ☐ Use enough facts and reasons. If you have time, add more.
- ☐ Restate your opinion in the conclusion. If you have not done this, do it now.

Proofreading Checklist
- ☐ Check the spellings of words. If you are not sure of one, use another word.
- ☐ Check for incomplete sentences. Give each the subject or verb that it needs.

Apply It ▶ Revise and proofread the draft of your test essay. Work right on the draft. Make the changes as neatly as you can.

▶ If this had been a real test, you would now turn your paper in to be graded. If you can, meet with a small group of students. Share your test essays. Discuss the process of writing a test essay. Which parts were difficult? Which parts seemed easier? Help each other to relax regarding test essays. Giving one another suggestions for improving your test essays.

CHAPTER 2 Writing an Advertisement

What ads in newspapers or magazines have caught your eye? Clever words and dramatic pictures often work together in ads. They attract the audience's attention.

Writing catchy advertisements is a great career for someone who has skills in persuasive writing. After all, an advertisement has one main purpose: to persuade the audience to buy the product!

What to Do   Learn the key elements of a successful ad.

- Headlines that grab the audience's attention
- A photograph or drawing to identify the product
- Facts and details about the product
- Details that appeal to the audience's needs and interests
- Persuasive words to encourage the audience to buy the product
- Suggestions about how or where the audience might buy the product

How to Do It   Study this advertisement, written by a group of students. Note the key elements.

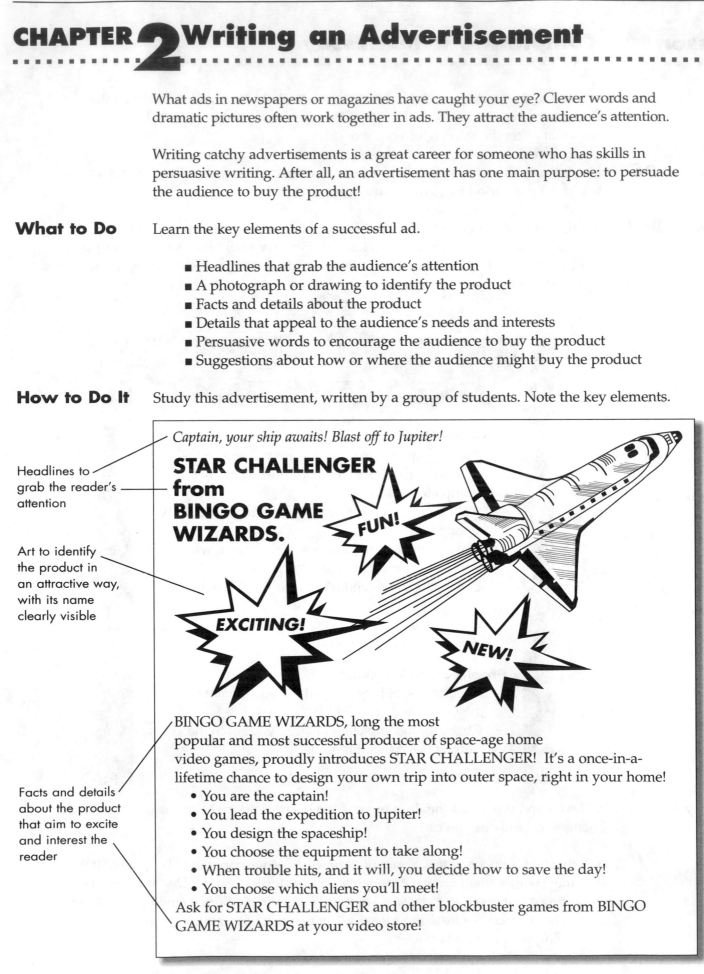

Headlines to grab the reader's attention

Art to identify the product in an attractive way, with its name clearly visible

Facts and details about the product that aim to excite and interest the reader

Captain, your ship awaits! Blast off to Jupiter!

STAR CHALLENGER from BINGO GAME WIZARDS.

FUN!

EXCITING!

NEW!

BINGO GAME WIZARDS, long the most popular and most successful producer of space-age home video games, proudly introduces STAR CHALLENGER! It's a once-in-a-lifetime chance to design your own trip into outer space, right in your home!
- You are the captain!
- You lead the expedition to Jupiter!
- You design the spaceship!
- You choose the equipment to take along!
- When trouble hits, and it will, you decide how to save the day!
- You choose which aliens you'll meet!
Ask for STAR CHALLENGER and other blockbuster games from BINGO GAME WIZARDS at your video store!

Review It

▶ Answer the following questions about the advertisement on page 68.

1. What type of product is advertised?

_____

2. What is the product's name?

_____

3. What company makes it?

_____

4. What are two specific details about the product?

_____

_____

5. What audience did the writers of this ad have in mind? Describe the audience (age, interests, and so on) as you imagine it.

_____

_____

6. What are two examples of persuasive words or phrases that the writer used to appeal to the audience's interests?

_____

_____

7. What suggestions does the ad provide to help the audience buy the product?

_____

_____

Apply It

▶ For this project, you might work alone, with a partner, or with a small group. Flip through magazines and newspapers, looking at ads. Clip the ones that are especially persuasive. Save them in your notebook.

▶ Then think of a product you might write an ad for. It could be a totally new product, like a robot that does homework or a car with wings. It could be a new brand of a product that already exists, like a new kind of sports shoe.

▶ Brainstorm for ten minutes, jotting down every product idea that comes to you. Then choose one product as the topic for your ad.

Lesson 1   Targeting the Audience

Writers who work in the advertising business are called copywriters. Copywriters know that they must direct their ads to their target audience. First, they identify who the buyers will most likely be. Then they create ads that will appeal directly to those people.

What to Do

Now that you have chosen a product, take some time to think about the people who might buy it. Think about these questions:

- What makes your product special? What makes it different from other products of its type?
- What features will buyers like?
- What audience will this product especially appeal to? Think about their age and interests.
- For what reasons will the product appeal especially to this audience?

How to Do It

List features to match your audience. These will become the details that you use in your ad.

Often, copywriters use a product profile chart to list details that will match the wants, needs, and interests of the audience. Here is a product profile chart for the Star Challenger video game.

Product: Star Challenger home video game	
Target Audience: home video game players, age 12 and up	
Audience Interests, Wants, Needs	**Product Features to Match Audience**
They are interested in adventure.	They get to take exciting trips into outer space.
They want to be involved with the action.	They are characters in the game and can make choices.
They want to feel in charge or to feel like heroes.	The player is the captain of the voyage.
They want to win a contest or face a challenge.	The trip takes dangerous twists and turns, and players meet some strange alien creatures.

Apply It

▶ Make your own product profile chart. Start the chart by using the answers you wrote at the start of this lesson. Add any new ideas that come to you. Think about the features of your product that will match the interests, wants, and needs of your audience.

Lesson 2 Using Connotations

Every word has a specific meaning. A word might also have a suggested meaning, or tone. The tone of the word might be positive or negative. The tone of a word is called its connotation.

What to Do

To persuade your audience to buy, you need to provide them with facts and details about the product. You also need to present those facts and details in the most positive way you can. Choose your words carefully. Use words that have positive connotations.

For example, the word *thin* has a specific meaning. It means "slim, not fat." Here are some other words that have meanings similar to the meaning of *thin*. Note how they have different connotations.

Word	Meaning	Connotation
slender	thin	positive
skinny	thin	negative
willowy	thin	positive
scrawny	thin	negative

How to Do It

The writer of the Star Challenger video game ad used this diagram to come up with words with positive connotations.

First, she listed details she wanted to include in her ad. Then she jotted down descriptive words and phrases about each detail. She wrote down every word and phrase that came to mind. Then she checked the words that she felt had positive connotations. She crossed out those that might have negative connotations. Here is part of her diagram.

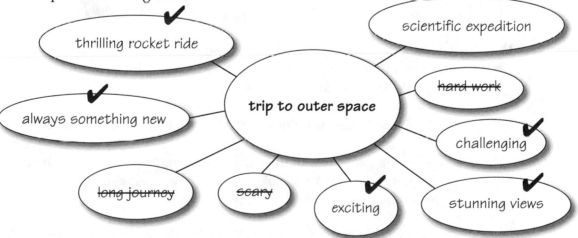

Apply It

▶ On a separate sheet of paper, create your own positive words diagram for the features of your product.

▶ For each feature of your product, jot down descriptive words and phrases. Check the words and phrases that have positive connotations. Cross out any that may sound negative to your audience.

Lesson 3 Drafting Your Advertisement

Now you are ready to draft your ad. Along with the writing, you will also need to sketch your artwork.

What to Do

First, plan your layout. The layout is the way you will set up your page. Get out some scratch paper and make sketches of possible layouts. Use circles and boxes to show the spaces you will use for blocks of text and pieces of art. Here is an example of a layout sketch.

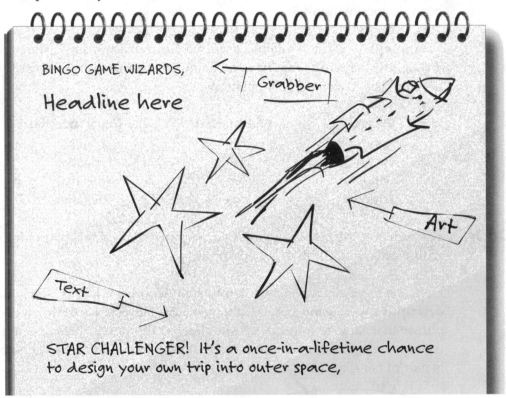

How to Do It

When planning your layout, you may want to use the following plan. Experiment with many different layouts until you are satisfied with the way your ad will look on the page. Be as creative as you can!

- Grabber: Create headlines that grab the audience's attention.

- Art: A large portion of the page should contain a picture of the product, with its name clearly visible. You may wish to include people using and enjoying the product.

- Main Text: Write your facts and details. Use words and phrases with positive connotations. Get your audience excited and interested!

Apply It

▶ Write and sketch your draft. Use your notes from Lessons 1 and 2 to write the draft of your ad. Use your layout plan to place the text and art on your page. Do not worry about the roughness of your artwork right now. Later, you will make the final copy of your ad.

Lesson 4 Completing Your Advertisement

Finish your ad by revising the text and the art. When it is ready for the public, put it to the test. See whether people are interested enough to want to buy the product.

What to Do

If you are working with a group, draw on everyone's skills and talents. Have the best writers revise and proofread the copy. Have the best artists revise and polish the art. Have the whole group brainstorm better headlines.

If you are working alone, try to "step back" from your work and look at it the way someone else would.

How to Do It

Use the revision checklist on page 35. Use the proofreading checklist on page 36. Also use the checklists below, which focus on key elements and proofreading problems in an advertisement for a product.

Revision Checklist
- ☐ The headlines should grab the audience's attention. Use more exciting words if you can.
- ☐ The details should appeal to your target audience. Replace details if they do not.
- ☐ Use words with positive connotations. Replace any that seem negative *for your audience*.
- ☐ Use art that shows the product in a positive way. Replace it if it does not.
- ☐ The page layout should make the most important parts of the ad stand out. Move the parts around to make them work together.

Proofreading Checklist
- ☐ Check the spellings of words that describe the product.
- ☐ Check the guide to grammar, mechanics, and usage on pages 76–80.

Apply It

▶ Test your ad before you revise it. Advertising writers always "test" their ads on a small group of people in their target audience. They show the ad to the sample audience and ask for feedback. Meet with a small group of classmates. Have the group members be your sample audience. Share ideas and suggestions with each other to make your ads even better. Make any changes that seem to be needed.

▶ Then go through the revision checklists. When you are satisfied with your ad, make the final copy. Use bright paints or colored pencils to make your artwork look exciting.

What Have You Learned in Unit 4?

Use these questions to gather and review your thoughts about the writing you did in Unit 4. Don't worry about writing complete sentences. Just put some thoughts, ideas, and reactions down for each question.

Test Essay

1. What is a test essay prompt?

_____

2. What should you look for in a test essay prompt?

_____

3. How can you quickly organize your thoughts for a test essay?

_____

4. Why should you stop drafting a few minutes before the deadline?

_____

5. Why is it a good idea to use your strongest reason first in a test essay?

_____

Advertisement for a Product

6. What is the purpose of an advertisement for a product?

_____

7. Why is it important to think about the audience for an ad?

_____

8. What are connotations of words?

_____

9. Why would you use words with positive connotations in an ad?

_____

10. Why is it a good idea to test an ad with an audience?

_____

▶ If you can, share your answers with a partner or group. Talk about the ideas and experiences you had. Share problems and successes you had while writing. Develop a group list of tips for each kind of writing you did in this unit.

The Writing Process

The writing process

What happens when a writer turns words into a story or an essay? He or she follows a set of steps, from start to finish. These steps make up the writing process. If you follow the same steps, you can make the process work for you.

What is a process?

A process is a series of steps that lead to a goal. Each step brings the process closer to the goal. Suppose you wanted to grow a pepper plant in a pot. Growing a plant is a process. You choose seeds, plant them, water the plants, and pull weeds. Each step gets you closer to your goal, and finally you pick the peppers.

What is the writing process?

There are five main steps in the writing process. They are prewriting, drafting, revising, proofreading, and publishing. This chart shows them. You won't always follow them in order, and you may move back and forth between stages.

Prewriting

In prewriting, you decide what to write. This step is like deciding what seeds to grow. You explore your idea. You think about it and gather information about it. You organize your ideas. You think about the people you will be writing for. You decide what they need to know and how you want to tell it to them.

Drafting

In drafting, you put your ideas into words. You shape your words into sentences. You build your sentences into paragraphs. As you draft, you do not have to worry about parts that are not quite right. You will fix them in the next stage.

Revising

In revising, you improve your draft. You look for weak spots, such as a word that is not quite right. You make changes, or revisions, to strengthen those spots. Notice that the arrows in the drafting and revising sections can lead you back and forth. This part of the process is like watering and weeding in the growing process.

Proofreading

When you are satisfied with your revised work, you turn to proofreading. This stage is sometimes called editing. In this step, you check for and correct any errors you may have made in grammar, usage, and mechanics, including spelling.

Publishing

Finally, in the publishing stage, you make a final copy and publish it or share it with an audience.

A Guide for Writers: Grammar, Mechanics, and Usage

GRAMMAR

Nouns A **noun** is the name of a person, place, or thing. A **common noun** names any person, place, or thing. A **proper noun** names a particular person, place, or thing.

Common Nouns	Proper Nouns
ballplayer	Cal Ripken
city	Los Angeles
river	Hudson River
country	Peru
street	Jackson Avenue

Pronouns Pronouns are words that stand for or take the place of nouns.
The subject pronouns are:

Singular	Plural
I	we
you	you
he	they
she	they
it	they

Use a **subject pronoun** as the subject of a sentence.

Incorrect
Her and Rosa will be here soon.
Revision
She and Rosa will be here soon.

Use **subject pronouns** after the linking verb *to be*.

Incorrect
The winners were Leroy and him.
Revision
The winners were Leroy and he.

The object pronouns are:

Singular	Plural
me	us
you	you
him	them
her	them
it	them

Use **object pronouns** as the direct objects of sentences. A direct object receives the action in a sentence.

Incorrect
Rosa will call Leo and I.
Revision
Rosa will call Leo and me.

Use object pronouns as objects of prepositions. The object of a preposition is a noun or pronoun at the end of a prepositional phrase. (See **Prepositions**.)

Incorrect
Selena wrote to Duane and I.
Revision
Selena wrote to Duane and me.

Possessive pronouns show ownership. The possessive pronouns are:

Singular	Plural
my	our
your	your
his	their
her	their
its	their

Verbs A **verb** is a word that shows action or the fact that something exists. Verbs change form to show time. These forms are called *tenses*.

Use **irregular verbs** correctly. Some verbs have unusual forms for showing that an action happened in the past. When in doubt, check a dictionary or ask a good editor (such as your teacher).

Incorrect
The group sung their hits.
Revision
The group sang their hits.

Adjectives An **adjective** is a word used to describe a noun or pronoun. A **proper adjective** is made from a proper noun. It names a particular person, place, or thing.

Use the correct form to compare adjectives. To compare two persons, places, or things, use the **comparative** form. Add *-er* to most short adjectives. Use *more* with longer adjectives. Use one or the other, not both.

Incorrect	Revision
more long movie	longer movie
thrillinger movie	more thrilling movie
more newer movie	newer movie

To compare more than two persons, places, or things, use the **superlative** form. Add *-est* to most short adjectives. Use *most* with longer adjectives. Use one or the other, not both.

Incorrect	Revision
most slow bus	slowest bus
comfortablest bus	most comfortable bus
most noisiest bus	noisiest bus

Some adjectives use different words for comparisons.

Examples

bad	worse	worst
good	better	best

Adverbs An **adverb** is a word that modifies a verb, an adjective, or another adverb.

Do not use an adjective when you need an adverb.

Incorrect	Revision
We did the job good.	We did the job well.
We did it quick.	We did it quickly.

Use the correct form to compare adverbs. To compare two actions, use the **comparative form**. Add *-er* to most short adverbs. Use *more* with most adverbs. Use one or the other, not both.

Incorrect	Revision
spoke more softlier	spoke more softly
started more later	started later

To compare more than two actions, use the **superlative form**. Use *-est* with some short adverbs. Use *most* with most adverbs. Use one or the other, not both.

Incorrect	Revision
spoke most softliest	spoke most softly
started most latest	started latest

Some adverbs use different words for comparisons.

Examples

badly	worse	worst
well	better	best

Prepositions A **preposition** is a word that relates the noun or pronoun following it to another word in the sentence.

Examples

in	on	off	of	under
over	along	beside	above	between

I saw the funnel of a tornado in the distance. The funnel was moving in my direction.

Sentences A **sentence** is a group of words with two main parts: a complete subject and a complete predicate. Together these parts express a complete thought.

Use complete sentences, not **fragments**. A complete sentence has a subject and a verb. A fragment is missing one of those parts. Correct a fragment by adding the missing part.

Fragment
The book written by Gary Soto.
Revision
The book was written by Gary Soto.
Fragment
Because the rain finally stopped.
Revision
We went out because the rain finally stopped.

Avoid **run-on sentences**. A run-on sentence is really more than one sentence. Correct a run-on sentence by dividing it into two (or more) sentences.

Run-on
For months I saved all the money I earned, and I never spent any of it, and finally I had enough for the class trip.
Revision
For months I saved all the money I earned. I never spent any of it. Finally I had enough for the class trip.

Subject-Verb Agreement Make the subject and verb of a sentence agree in number. To make a subject and verb agree, make sure that both are **singular** or both are **plural**. A singular subject names one person, place, or thing. A plural subject names more than one person, place, or thing.

> **Incorrect**
> Some parts is missing.
> **Revision**
> Some parts are missing.

Be careful when a **prepositional phrase** comes between the subject and the verb. The verb must agree with the subject, not with the object of the preposition.

> **Incorrect**
> One of the parts are missing.
> **Revision**
> One of the parts is missing.

The pronoun *I* is singular, but it nearly always takes the plural form of a verb. (The only exceptions are *am* and *was*, which are singular forms of the verb *to be*.)

> **Incorrect**
> I urges you to act now.
> **Revision**
> I urge you to act now.
> **Incorrect**
> I is nearly ready.
> **Revision**
> I am nearly ready.

Phrases A **phrase** is a group of words, without a subject and verb, that works in a sentence as one part of speech.

A **prepositional phrase** is a group of words that includes a **preposition** and the **object of the preposition**, a noun or pronoun. The whole phrase works like an adjective or adverb. It modifies the meaning of another word or group of words.

Keep prepositions and their phrases close to the words they modify. Your sentence may not say what you mean if a prepositional phrase is in the wrong place.

> **One Meaning**
> The car with stripes looks great.
> (but another car does not)
> **Another Meaning**
> The car looks great with stripes.
> (but not without stripes)

Negatives A **negative** is a word or word part that means "not." The word *not* itself is a negative. So are *nobody* and *nowhere*. The contraction *-n't* is made from *not*. When *-n't* is part of a word, it is a negative.

Use only one negative in a sentence. More than one negative in a sentence is a "double negative." Remove double negatives in your sentences.

> **Incorrect**
> We don't have no blank cassettes.
> **Revision**
> We don't have any blank cassettes.
> We have no blank cassettes.

MECHANICS

Capitalization Capitalize the first word of a sentence.

> **Incorrect**
> the sun looked like an orange.
> **Revision**
> The sun looked like an orange.

Capitalize proper nouns.

> | **Incorrect** | **Revision** |
> | --- | --- |
> | boston red sox | Boston Red Sox |
> | ernesto galarza | Ernesto Galarza |
> | thailand | Thailand |

Capitalize proper adjectives.

> **Incorrect**
> foreign and american cars
> **Revision**
> foreign and American cars

Capitalize the first word and all important words in titles of books, movies, and other works of art.

> | **Incorrect** | **Revision** |
> | --- | --- |
> | *Jurassic park* | *Jurassic Park* |

Capitalize a person's title when it is followed by the person's name.

> | **Incorrect** | **Revision** |
> | --- | --- |
> | senator Marston | Senator Marston |

Punctuation

End Marks Use an end mark at the end of

every sentence. Use a period to end a sentence that makes a statement or gives a command. Use a question mark to end a question. Use an exclamation point after a statement showing strong emotion.

Incorrect
This is the movie to see
Have you seen it already
Yes, and it's great
Revisions
This is the movie to see.
Have you seen it already?
Yes, and it's great!

Commas Use a comma between the two independent clauses in a compound sentence.

Incorrect
Levon was standing in the doorway and his brother was sitting on the sofa.
Revision
Levon was standing in the doorway, and his brother was sitting on the sofa.

Use commas to separate three or more words in a series.

Incorrect
I bought a shirt a cap and a compact disc.
Revision
I bought a shirt, a cap, and a compact disc.

Use commas to set the rest of the sentence apart from the spoken words in a direct quotation.

Incorrect
She said "I'm not ready."
"Wait here" he said "until I return."
Revision
She said, "I'm not ready."
"Wait here," he said, "until I return."

Quotation Marks A direct quotation represents a person's exact words. Use quotation marks around the words the speaker says.

Incorrect
Mr. Hsu said, Take tomorrow off.
Revision
Mr. Hsu said, "Take tomorrow off."

When you use a comma or a period with a direct quotation, place it inside the final quotation mark.

Incorrect
"I'll see you tomorrow", I said.
She said, "I'll be waiting".
Revision
"I'll see you tomorrow," I said.
She said, "I'll be waiting."

When you use a question mark or exclamation point with a direct quotation, place it inside the quotation marks if it goes with the speaker's words.

Incorrect
I called, "Is anybody home"?
A voice answered, "I'll be right there"!
Revision
I called, "Is anybody home?"
A voice answered, "I'll be right there!"

Dialogue is written conversation. When you write dialogue, start a new paragraph each time the speaker changes. Begin a new paragraph each time a different person speaks.

Incorrect
"Good morning," he said. "Says who?" I answered.
Revision
"Good morning," he said.
"Says who?" I answered.

Apostrophes A possessive noun shows ownership, as *Luis's* does in *Luis's dog*. To make a singular noun possessive, add an apostrophe (') and an *s*, no matter what letter ends the noun.

Noun	Possessive
student	student's
boss	boss's

To make a plural noun possessive, add an apostrophe and an *s* if the noun ends with some letter other than *s*. Add only an apostrophe if the noun ends with *s*.

Noun	Possessive
children	children's
students	students'
families	families'
lawyers	lawyers'

Possessive pronouns show ownership, like possessive nouns. However, possessive pronouns are not spelled with apostrophes.

Incorrect
Those snapshots are their's.
The dog ate it's food.

Revision
Those snapshots are theirs.
The dog ate its food.

USAGE

bad, badly Use *bad* after linking verbs, such as *feel*, *look*, and *seem*. Use *badly* whenever an adverb is needed.

Incorrect
I felt badly about not being able to play in the game.

Revision
I felt bad about not being able to play in the game.

beside, besides Do not confuse these two prepositions, which have different meanings. Beside means "at the side of" or "close to." Besides means "in addition to."

Incorrect
I wondered whether anyone would be going on the trip beside the usual group.

Revision
I wondered whether anyone would be going on the trip besides the usual group.

can, may The verb *can* generally refers to the ability to do something. The verb *may* generally refers to permission to do something.

Incorrect
"Can I have the last hamburger?" he asked.

Revision
"May I have the last hamburger?" he asked.

good, well Use the predicate adjective *good* after linking verbs, such as *feel*, *look*, *smell*, *taste*, and *seem*. Use *well* whenever you need an adverb.

Incorrect
We hadn't won the game, but we could hold our heads high because we knew that we played good.

Revision
We hadn't won the game, but we could hold our heads high because we knew that we played well.

its, it's Do not confuse the possessive pronoun *its* with the contraction *it's*, standing for *it is* or *it has*.

Incorrect
That dog has something stuck in it's paw.

Revision
That dog has something stuck in its paw.

of, have Do not use *of* in place of *have* after auxiliary verbs, such as *would*, *could*, *should*, *may*, *might*, or *must*.

Incorrect
You should of seen the way Hakeem went up for the rebound.

Revision
You should have seen the way Hakeem went up for the rebound.

than, then The conjunction *than* is used to connect the two parts of a comparison. Do not confuse *than* with the adverb *then*, which usually refers to time.

Incorrect
My brother is exactly a year older then I am.

Revision
My brother is exactly a year older than I am.

their, there, they're Do not confuse the spellings of these three words. *Their* is a possessive pronoun and always modifies a noun. *There* is usually used either at the beginning of a sentence or as an adverb. *They're* is a contraction for *they are*.

Incorrect
"Are those they're sweat pants?" I asked. "No," he said. "There over their, behind the lockers."

Revision
"Are those their sweat pants?" I asked. "No," he said. "They're over there, behind the lockers."